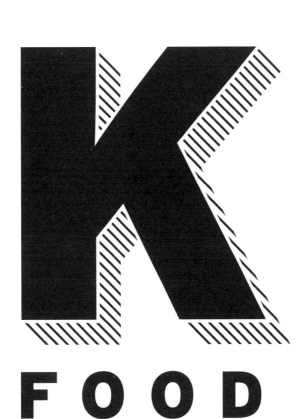

K

FOOD

*Korean home cooking
and street food*

DA-HAE AND GARETH WEST

MITCHELL BEAZLEY

CONTENTS

YOU HAVE TO

measure it

TO KNOW IF IT'S

TOO LONG OR

too short

긴 짧은

Mostly about my mom...

I was born in Busan, South Korea, but moved to England when I was three. Raised by my Korean mom and English dad, I couldn't really speak much English when we first moved here. When my mom dropped me off at nursery school for the first time, she worried about how I'd interact with the other kids with the language barrier. Fortunately, kids are kids and just get on with it, creating strong bonds over toys, cookies, and nap times. So, things actually turned out pretty well and language was never an issue.

It was incredibly important to my mom that I knew about the country that I came from, and I think this is why I was so proud of being Korean when I first started school. I'd write my name in scrawly Korean on top of all my schoolwork (it was even mentioned in one of my school reports), and I'd always be the first to point out where Korea was on the world map.

My dad traveled a lot on business, so whenever it was just my mom and me at home, we'd have Korean food for breakfast, lunch, and supper. Having eaten rice and *kimchi* for every meal since she was young, it was initially difficult for my mom to adapt to Western foods. Every time we visited Korea, she'd make sure to bring back enough bags of dried anchovies and *gochugaru* (Korean red chile powder) in her suitcase to last us until our next trip. It was difficult to get Korean ingredients in the UK back then, so my resourceful mom would adapt recipes so that she could use the ingredients she could get hold of, along with the ones she'd snuck back in her suitcase. *Kkakdugi*, a Korean radish *kimchi* was made with turnips in our house, *gochujang* (Korean red chile paste) was homemade (there are photos of a three- to four-year-old me, licking it off my hands and elbows), and my mom would also forage for the tips of wild fern (often eaten in *bibimbap*) and young rapeseed leaves to make her summer *kimchis*. Gradually, my mom took more interest in cooking other foods and, little by little, she learned more about different non-Korean ingredients. Soon enough, Korean food became just one of many types of cuisine we enjoyed at home (much to my dad's relief).

While I was growing up in the UK, Korea went through some really tough economic times and was hit hard by the IMF crisis. Things looked pretty bleak for the country, but my mom was insistent that one day Korea would develop this great big economy that other countries would aspire to. She'd try to push to me the importance of learning Korean, but going through my trickier teenage years, I took little interest in my lessons. They felt like a waste of time because, back then—at least to me—it looked like Korea was always going to be this small, hidden country that no one knew anything about.

Despite my disregard for my Korean lessons, I did look forward to our trips to Korea, and I was lucky enough to visit pretty often while I was growing up. Visits were packed full of rushing around to visit relatives, eating lots, and revisiting my mom's childhood haunts. But in hindsight, it was the everyday things I loved most. Going to the market with my mom was so different from going to the markets in the UK, and filled with such sights, sounds, smells, and hustle and bustle. I remember going to the beach with my cousins, going fishing, and swimming in the bath houses. I'm so thankful to have so many childhood memories there.

There was one particular vacation, though, that really cemented Korea as a second home for me. It was during one summer while I was at university, and I went (slightly under duress at the time) to spend a few months living with my cousin Jisoo on Jeju Island. Jeju Island is the honeymoon destination of Korea and for good reason—a volcanic island full of mountains, surrounded by

crystal blue seas and with its own sunny microclimate, which is warmer than the rest of Korea. It's impossible not to fall in love with it. I grew a whole new appreciation of Korea that I'd never had before. That summer was one of the best vacations I've ever had. Jisoo and I had such fun swimming, watching Korean dramas, ordering takeouts, and eating Baskin Robbins until late into the night. It was the longest time I'd ever spent in Korea since moving to the UK, and I loved it.

Ever since that summer in Jeju, I started to take a lot more interest in Korea. I started speaking to my mom in Korean (she had persistently never given up trying) and I started to seek out more and more information about the country, and particularly the food. As I've grown up, I've seen Korea go from strength to strength and I couldn't help but sit up and take notice when Korean food and flavors started to creep onto small segments on TV and appear in fancy restaurant menus. Somewhere in the back of my mind, I wanted to be part of this—to link back to my Korean roots and promote the food I loved. I just didn't know how or where to begin.

IT ALL STARTED WITH A McDONALD'S...

Gareth and I met through mutual friends in my last year of university and one of the reasons we got along so well from the beginning was because of our shared love of food. Gareth has always loved food. All food, really. When he was growing up, he never watched much children's TV and instead was always fixated on cooking shows. He loved cooking and probably would have made a great chef (I think), but he'd never thought of doing it as a career. Instead, one of his first jobs was working at a pub and from there he worked his way up through hospitality until he reached the head offices of the restaurant group D&D London.

We got married in 2012 and went to Korea on our honeymoon. We'd spent several days with my family, feasting on huge Korean dinners, with Gareth proclaiming that everything he ate was his new favorite dish. It was his first time in Korea and he hadn't known what to expect, but he was completely blown away by it all—and particularly the food.

In the past, it had always been difficult to try any sort of non-Korean food in Korea. Korea is full of really great Korean restaurants (most of which specialize in just one dish) but had resisted much culinary influence from other countries. Despite this, for as long as I can remember, it's always been possible to get a *bulgogi* burger at any one of the fast-food restaurants. One night, we were walking from my aunt's house to our nearby hotel, when we wandered past a McDonald's. Like most global fast-food chains, McDonald's adapts their menu to the country that they're in, and in Korea, they have a *bulgogi* burger. It's a

standard McDonald's beef burger that's marinated in a sweet, sticky soy glaze based on the Korean BBQ marinade. I'd told Gareth about this Korean twist on their burgers, and he was insistent that we try one. It wasn't the best burger that Gareth had ever eaten (though it was the best he'd ever had at McDonald's), but the idea of marrying those Korean flavors with Western-style food stuck in our heads.

When we returned to England, we decided to try making some *bulgogi* burgers at home. They turned out better than we'd ever imagined, with the sweet, salty *bulgogi* marinade teasing the meaty flavors out of the burgers. Gareth ended up eating three in one sitting. As we ate them, we kept saying that if someone sold them in the UK, they'd be a real hit. Then it struck us. Why couldn't that be us?

The more we thought about starting a Korean burger business together, the more it made sense. After those first *bulgogi* burgers we made at home, we started putting some plans together, finding some fantastic suppliers, and testing lots of new recipes. Eight months later we traded at our first market as Busan BBQ.

Since starting Busan BBQ, we've been back to Korea a few times and have seen how the food is really starting to change there. Though great Korean food can still be found everywhere you look, there's been a wave of fusion Korean restaurants that have opened, which take Korean flavors and mash them with different cuisines. A lot of Korean Americans have taken the foods that they've grown up with and brought them back to Korea, and young Koreans are excited by the change.

Similarly, when we started Busan BBQ, very few people had heard of Korean food. We'd offer *kimchi* on our burgers and would have to explain what it was to almost every customer. Now, we can go easily go through 45 pounds of it in a weekend, with customers asking for more. There's been an explosion of interest in Korean cooking and ingredients over the past year or so, and we're so proud to be part of that.

This book is a combination of the recipes I've grown up with along with new recipes that we've thought up along the way. Some of the recipes might not be as authentic as you'd imagine, but then, what is authentic nowadays, anyway? This is Korean cooking as we know it—the kind of food that's often thrown together to create something delicious. This is the food we love and we hope you'll love it too.

Essential Korean Ingredients

Failure
IS THE
Mother
OF ALL
Success

Korean food is predominantly based on a handful of ingredients, the most common of which are the jang, which are products that have been made from fermented soybeans. The jang include what I think of as the "holy trinity" of Korean cooking—gochujang, doenjang, and ganjang. Most dishes will contain at least one of these three ingredients.

Gochujang [1]
Gochujang is Korean red chile paste. Made from fermented soybean powder, sweet rice flour, and dried Korean red chiles, *gochujang* is sweet and spicy but has a real depth of flavor and an earthiness that's very unique.

Doenjang [2]
Often described as Korean miso, *doenjang* is a fermented soybean paste. Unlike miso, the paste is quite coarse, often containing whole beans, and the flavor is much saltier and punchier.

Ganjang [3 and 4]
Ganjang is soy sauce, and was originally a by-product of the *doenjang*-making process. Korean soy sauce is often slightly sweeter and more like caramel in flavor than other soy sauces. There are lots of different varieties of soy sauce, but the main two that we use in Korean cooking are *jin ganjang* [3], a regular soy sauce used for braising dishes, dipping sauces, and marinades and *guk ganjang* [4], a much paler, saltier soy sauce used in soups and to lightly flavor dishes such as *muchims* (see page 60).

KEY CUPBOARD INGREDIENTS
The *jangs* aside, there are a few other essentials that you'll need in your cupboard for Korean cooking. These include:

Gochugaru [5]
Gochugaru is often described as "Korean chile powder," "Korean red pepper powder," or "Korean red pepper flakes." Made from ground, dried Korean chiles, *gochugaru* comes in two types—fine or coarse. The fine *gochugaru* is used to make *gochujang*, while the coarse version is for everyday kitchen use. Whenever we mention *gochugaru* in this book, we're referring to these coarser flakes. *Gochugaru* is spicy but the chiles have a subtle, smoky sweetness to them. It is usually used when more heat is needed in a dish, rather than adding more *gochujang*. This is because adding too much *gochujang* can make a dish taste too salty whereas *gochugaru* just brings a little bit more spice.

Rice [6]

Koreans usually eat short-grain white rice (sushi rice), which has a high starch content that makes it sticky and shiny. Though most Korean dishes are based on sharing, everyone usually gets their own individual bowl of rice. Korean rice needs to be sticky, fluffy, and glossy, which can only achieved with the perfect ratio of water to rice (see page 26).

Roasted Sesame Oil [7]

It is really important to have a good-quality, roasted, 100 percent pure (not blended) sesame oil as part of your Korean larder. The good ones are pricier but are much stronger in flavor, and a little goes a really long way. Buying a cheap, blended version is a false economy because you end up having to use a lot more. Roasted sesame oil is not normally used for frying because it has a much lower burning point than cooking oils, such as vegetable oil, and is instead used in dipping sauces and marinades or to finish dishes, where it gives a creamy, nutty aroma.

Roasted Sesame Seeds [8]

Sesame seeds can be bought already roasted, or you can buy plain ones which you toast yourself in a dry skillet at home. You can buy black or white sesame seeds, but we usually use the white ones. These give a nice nutty texture and also look great sprinkled over a dish as a garnish.

Apple Vinegar [9]

We really like using apple vinegar. It has a distinctively fresh apple-y flavor that is tart and a little sweet. If you can't get hold of any, rice vinegar or apple cider vinegar also work as substitutes in any of the recipes where apple vinegar is used in this book.

Seaweed

There are lots of different types of seaweed and, quite confusingly, the same varieties are often sold under different names. The three that we use in this book are:

Gim (also known as "nori" or "sushi" seaweed) [10] These are square sheets of seaweed, usually used for sushi. Sometimes these sheets come seasoned with oil and salt. The seasoned seaweed is great cut into squares and eaten simply with rice, or cut into matchstick-thin strips as a garnish.

Miyuk (also known as "*wakame*") [11] These usually come dried in long, thin packs and are used for soup. A little goes a long way; as you rehydrate this seaweed in water it'll double in volume and go from crispy black strands to slippery green ribbons.

Dashima (also known as "*kombu*" or "*kelp*") [12] These are dried, tough sheets of seaweed, usually used for stock, which can be bought in long sheets or ready-cut. I normally use the ready cut-kind for ease. They often have a little bit of a white dusty coating on them but don't wash this off; this is where all the flavor is.

Noodles

Noodles form an important part of the Korean diet, and come in a variety of different types, from thin vermicelli noodles made from flour, to springy buckwheat noodles, cellophane noodles made from sweet potato, and last (but by no means least) the instant noodles, or *ramyun*, loved by all. For a detailed breakdown of noodle types, see page 162.

OTHER COMMON INGREDIENTS

In this book, you'll notice a few other ingredients that frequently pop up. These include:

Cabbage *Kimchi* [13]

As well as appearing as a side dish or *banchan* with almost every Korean meal, *kimchi* (see page 30) is often used for cooking. Cabbage *kimchi* is the most frequently used *kimchi* for cooking. However, it has to be matured for at least a few weeks to allow the flavors to deepen and intensify, making the *kimchi* tangy and strong.

Sweet Rice Flour [14]

Also known as glutinous rice flour, *chapssal garu*, or more commonly *mochiko*, sweet rice flour is used in the fermentation process of both *gochujang* and *kimchi* and is also commonly used as a thickener for sauces and in batters (such as for our Korean Fried Chicken, see page 212).

Dried Anchovies [15]

Usually found in the frozen section of Korean and Asian supermarkets, dried anchovies come in lots of different sizes. The two we've used in this book are the tiny anchovies (which are no bigger than a fingernail) for frying as a *banchan* (see page 44) and the large dried anchovies, which form a key ingredient in our stock recipe (see page 22).

Fermented Shrimp [16]

These teeny, tiny shrimp or *saeujeot* are preserved through salting and can be found in jars and in the frozen section of Korean and Asian supermarkets. A common ingredient in *kimchi*, they make a great seasoning. A word of warning: They're very salty, so a little goes a long way!

Fish Sauce [17]

Fish sauce is a key ingredient in *kimchi*. It smells very pungent and fishy if you're not used to it, but this mellows as you cook with it (or in the case of *kimchi*, once the dish has fermented and matured).

Mandu Skins

Mandu skins are traditionally used to wrap a variety of savory fillings and are then pan-fried, steamed, deep-fried, or added to soups. While knowing how to make these dumpling wrappers is by no means essential (they're so easy to find at any Chinese supermarket), you will get far more satisfaction from making your own (see page 24).

Mooli [18]

Though traditional Korean cooking would use Korean radishes, mooli are much easier to get hold of outside of Korea and taste quite similar. Mooli (also known as "white radish" or "daikon") are long white vegetables that can be found in most Asian supermarkets. They are much milder in flavor than the peppery red English breakfast radishes and add a great crunch and texture to salads and slaws, but are also used in soups to give them body and for their clean, refreshing flavor.

Scallions [19]

Scallions have been part of Korean cooking since long before the onion was introduced. They have a subtler flavor than normal onions. We often use the finely chopped green part as a garnish.

Garlic and Ginger Root [20 and 21]

These two ingredients are as important as each other in Korean cooking, and are probably the ingredients that we've used the most in this book. Korean cooking is often quite punchy, so garlic and ginger root are usually minced for maximum flavor.

Korean/Asian pear

Unlike the American pears we're used to seeing, Korean pears are large and round, with a thick papery golden skin. The skin is usually peeled and discarded, and the fruit inside is very crisp, sweet, and juicy. My favorite way to eat these is straight from the fridge, so that they're really cold and refreshing.

Yuja/Yuzu

Yuja (more commonly known as *Yuzu*) is a tangy citrus fruit with a slightly bitter edge, a little like a grapefruit. As a fresh fruit, it resembles a mandarin but it's easier to get hold of as a concentrate (usually in small 2¼fl oz bottles). *Yuja* has a lovely fresh scent and makes a delicious alternative to lemons.

Jujube

Also known as *daechu* in Korean, *jujube* are small, dried red dates with a sweet, earthy flavor that can be used in either desserts or savory dishes. In Korea, they're known for their medicinal properties and are often sliced thinly to add to teas or used for cooking in dishes such as *sam gye tang*.

HOMEMADE STOCKS AND DIPPING SAUCES

There are a few basic stock and dipping-sauce recipes that you'll need to have up your sleeve. As you make your way through this book, you'll notice that you're constantly referred back to this section since they provide the backbone of a lot of Korean recipes.

Stocks

One of the most important basics stocks is *Myeulchi Gookmul* (see page 22), a mild, but deeply flavored stock made from dried anchovies and kelp, which provides the base for most Korean soups and stews. I do have something of a cheat's confession to make, though; there are times when I don't always have dried anchovies at home, or I'm tired and don't want to bother with boiling up a new batch of stock. In these instances I use a light chicken or vegetable stock instead.

For the dishes that need big, meatier flavors, we've also included a recipe for a rich brown chicken stock (*Dak Yuksu*, see page 23), which is the perfect way to use up any carcasses from a leftover roast chicken, and is packed full of flavor.

Dipping Sauces

There are many overlaps when it comes to dipping sauces. Fried Korean dishes (of which there are many) can be quite heavy, and so need something tangy, such as our soy vinegar dipping sauce (*Cho Ganjang*, see page 21), to cut through the grease. Alternatively, some dishes just need a sauce so that everyone can season to their own taste, which is where our soy seasoning sauce (*Yangnyum Jang*, see page 21) comes in.

Cho Gochujang TANGY CHILE DIPPING SAUCE

Translating as "vinegared chile paste," *cho gochujang* is sweet and spicy with a tart edge. In Korea it is usually eaten as a dipping sauce for raw fish, known as *hwe*, and is also often used as an ingredient in *banchan* sharing dishes such as *miyuk cho muchim* (see page 61).

SERVES
4

3 tablespoons *gochujang* (Korean red chile paste)
1 tablespoon lemon juice
2 tablespoons apple vinegar

1 tablespoon superfine sugar
2 garlic cloves, minced

Mix all the ingredients together in a bowl until well combined, then serve in individual dipping bowls.

Supermarket Gochujang

Packed with salty, sweet umami flavor, *gochujang* brings both a unique heat and depth to anything you add it to, and is such an essential part of Korean cooking that other chile sauces and pastes, such as *sriracha* and *tobanjan*, just don't make very good substitutes. While we're lucky to live close to a number of Korean supermarkets, when we started putting this book together we realized it was important for us to create an easy-to-make *gochujang* from ingredients that you could get hold of in a good ordinary supermarket, because we know that not everyone has this luxury. This really does taste similar to the real thing. Make a batch and leave it in your refrigerator so that you always have some on hand.

MAKES
1
SMALL JAR

½ cup white miso paste
¼ cup corn syrup
¼ cup cayenne pepper

2 tablespoons mirin
1 tablespoon superfine sugar
1 garlic clove, minced

Mix all the ingredients together in a bowl until well combined. Decant into a sterilized jar and store in the refrigerator. It should keep for at least a month.

> **TIP:** This *gochujang* has something more of a fiery kick than the traditional variety, so if you're using it for cooking, reduce the quantities of the sauce slightly from what we've suggested (unless you like it hot, that is).

CHO GOCHUJANG

SSAMJANG

Ssamjang KOREAN BBQ DIPPING SAUCE

The "*ssam*" in *ssamjang* refers to the lettuce wraps used for Korean BBQ, which is what this sauce is usually eaten with. It's a mixture of *gochujang* and *doenjang*, so it's quite earthy, a little salty, and has a tiny amount of chile in it, making it perfect with barbecued meats. *Ssamjang* is also often eaten in Korea as a dipping sauce for raw vegetables, as well as forming the base sauce for our *Ssamjang Mayo* (see page 83).

SERVES 4

1 tablespoon *doenjang* (Korean soybean paste)
1 tablespoon *gochujang* (Korean red chile paste)

½ scallion, trimmed and finely chopped
2 garlic cloves, minced

1 teaspoon sesame oil
1 teaspoon sesame seeds

Put all the ingredients in a bowl and mix together well,
then serve in individual dipping bowls.

Yangnyum Jang SOY SEASONING SAUCE

With its salty, slightly spicy kick, this sauce can be found in every noodle house in Korea.

SERVES 4

⅓ cup regular soy sauce
1 tablespoon fish sauce
2 scallions, trimmed and finely chopped

2 bird's-eye chiles, trimmed and finely chopped
2 tablespoons *gochugaru* (Korean red chile powder)
1 tablespoon water

1 teaspoon superfine sugar
2 garlic cloves, minced

Mix all the ingredients together in a small serving bowl
until well combined. Transfer to the middle of the table
and serve with a bowl of *Kalguksu* (see page 173) or
some simply steamed tofu.

Cho Ganjang SOY VINEGAR DIPPING SAUCE

Cho ganjang literally translates as "vinegared soy sauce," with "*cho*" referring to "vinegar" and "*ganjang*" the Korean word for "soy sauce." It's amazing how a little vinegar can transform this sauce—it lightens it and gives it a really nice tanginess that works really well with fried dishes, such as *Haemul Pajeon* (see page 54), or with simple dumplings, such as *Gogi Mandu* (see page 53).

SERVES 4

¼ cup dark soy sauce
2 tablespoons apple vinegar
4 teaspoons *gochugaru* (Korean red chile powder)

Put all the ingredients in a bowl and mix together well,
then serve in individual dipping bowls.

Myeulchi Gookmul ANCHOVY STOCK

Knowing how to prepare your own anchovy stock is a basic essential when it comes to Korean cooking, and it's so easy to make. It doesn't taste overly fishy since the anchovies are just dried and not salted, but it gives a really clean, deep savory flavour to the many soups and stews in which it's used.

MAKES ABOUT
3 pints

¾lb mooli, cut into 2-inch pieces
1 onion, coarsely chopped
2 scallions, trimmed and coarsely chopped
4 whole garlic cloves

4¼ pints water, divided
15 large dried anchovies, halved and gutted
5 x 2-inch *dashima (kombu)* kelp squares

1_ Put the mooli, onion, scallions, garlic cloves, and ½ of the measurement water in a large saucepan or stockpot. Bring to a boil, then reduce the heat and continue to simmer for 20 minutes.

2_ Add the anchovies to the pot along with the kelp squares and the remaining water, return to a boil, and cook for a further 20 minutes, skimming off and discarding any foam from the top of the stock with a slotted spoon as you go, until the liquid is a light brown. Remove from the heat and let cool.

3_ Once cool, strain the stock through a colander to remove the vegetables. Use immediately or pour into a suitable resealable container and refrigerate for up to two days, or freeze for longer.

Dak Yuksu RICH BROWN CHICKEN STOCK

While most Korean soups and stews are traditionally made using the anchovy stock *Myeulchi Gookmul* (see opposite) as a base, I actually think this brown chicken stock works just as well because it's so rich and full of flavor. If you've roasted a chicken, this is a great way to use the leftovers. However, if you're using a whole chicken, remove the breasts and set them aside for another day, because you won't need the extra meat in this recipe.

MAKES ABOUT
2 pints

2¼lb chicken wings
2¾lb chicken, breasts removed, or the leftover carcass
   from a roasted chicken
3 tablespoons vegetable oil, divided, plus extra for greasing

2 large onions, coarsely sliced
pinch of salt
4 whole garlic cloves
7oz mooli, cut into 2-inch pieces

1_ Preheat the oven to 425°F.

2_ Use the heel of a large knife to carefully press down on the chicken wings, cracking the bones. Repeat with the spine of the carcass and the chicken legs.

3_ Place the bones on a large greased roasting pan, spoon over 2 tablespoons of the vegetable oil, and coat evenly. Roast for 45 minutes. Remove from the oven, skim off any fat that may have rendered down using a spoon, and set aside.

4_ Heat the remaining 1 tablespoon of oil in a large, heavy saucepan or stockpot. Add the onions and salt and cook gently over low heat, stirring occasionally, for 15 minutes or until the onions are golden brown and sticky.

5_ Add the garlic, mooli, and chicken bones to the pot along with any sticky pieces left on the bottom of the pan (these will be packed full of flavor). Add enough water to cover everything by about 1 inch and bring to a boil. Lower the heat and simmer gently for 2 hours, skimming off any foam or fat deposits that float to the top using a slotted spoon, and topping off the liquid with extra cold water if it drops below the level of the ingredients.

6_ Strain the solids from the liquid using a fine-mesh strainer or cheesecloth and let the stock cool for at least 20 minutes, then scoop off fat that may have collected on the top. Use immediately or freeze in a resealable container for later.

Homemade Mandu (Dumpling) Skins

Although dumpling skins are easy to get hold of at any Chinese supermarket—and if you can't find them you can always use wonton or gyoza wrappers instead—it's really simple and satisfying to make your own. Homemade skins are more pliable so you can fill them with more filling and, because they aren't so delicate, they're also more suitable for clumsy hands.

MAKES
22 to 24
DUMPLING
SKINS

1 cup all-purpose flour, plus extra for dusting
pinch of salt
¼ cup warm water, plus extra if needed

1_ Sift the flour into a large bowl, add the salt, and mix together. Stir in the warm water a little at a time, mixing with a wooden spoon, until the mixture starts to come together to form a dough (you may need to add an extra teaspoon or two of water).

2_ Turn the dough out onto a lightly floured surface and knead for 10 minutes, then seal in plastic wrap and let rest in the refrigerator for 20 minutes.

3_ Once it has rested, knead the dough for another 10 minutes until smooth and elastic.

4_ Shape the dough into a ball, then roll it out to a thickness of ¹/₁₆ inch. Cut out a circle using a 3¼-inch cookie cutter and set the trimmings aside. Repeat with the remaining dough pieces, lightly dusting each dough circle with a pinch of flour and covering loosely with platic wrap as you go. Gather together the excess dough, shape into a ball, and roll out to make more dumpling skins.

5_ Fill the dumpling skins with sweet or savory fillings and cook as per your chosen recipe, or freeze them to use later (see Tip).

TIP: *Mandu* freeze really well and are great for making in big batches; just be sure that you arrange them spaced well apart on a baking pan lined with plastic wrap for their initial freezing so that they don't stick to one another. Once frozen they can be stacked. *Mandu* don't need to be defrosted before cooking—you just need to cook them for a little longer to make sure the filling is cooked through and the skins are browned.

How to Cook Rice the Korean Way

Cooking rice is actually a lot easier than most people think. This way of measuring the water vs. rice ratio will work for rice cookers, pressure cookers, and saucepans. This is the way that most Koreans cook their rice, so here's the secret:

1_ Put ½ cup uncooked short-grain rice per person into a large saucepan, making sure the rice sufficiently covers the bottom of your saucepan (so this works better for a minimum of 2 people). Fill the pan with enough water to cover. Rub the rice between your fingers in the water to wash off the excess starch, then drain off the water. Repeat at least twice more until the water runs clear.

2_ Smooth out the rice so that the surface is even, then lay your hand flat on top of the rice.

3_ Leaving your hand flat against the rice, fill the pan with water, until the water level reaches your knuckle (this will be about ¾ inch above the rice).

4_ Place the saucepan over high heat, cover with a lid, and cook for 8 minutes. Then reduce the heat to low and cook for another 2 minutes.

5_ Turn the heat off and leave the saucepan, covered, for 10 minutes. Try to resist sneaking a peak at this stage—you don't want to release the steam from the pan.

6_ Once the rice has finished steaming, use a plastic rice spoon to separate the rice grains so that the rice is nice and fluffy.

TIP: If you have an electric stove, this method might need a little tweaking and playing around with since the burners hold their heat. When you reach step 5, move the pan onto a cold burner so that the residual heat doesn't scorch the bottom of the pan.

Kimchi

02

EVEN THE

Monkey

FALLS

FROM THE

TREE

You can't have a Korean meal without the country's favorite side, kimchi. An essential banchan or sharing dish, as well as an important ingredient in cooking, kimchi is so central to the Korean diet that it is eaten for breakfast, lunch, and dinner. In fact, most Koreans even have a kimchi refrigerator in their apartment to store their kimchi at a cool temperature (and to avoid everything else in their refrigerator taking on the strong kimchi flavor).

Traditionally a way of preserving vegetables for their nutrients in preparation for the long, harsh Korean winter, *kimchi* has been around in different guises as part of the Korean diet for centuries. When it was first made, vegetables were simply salted without any chiles (chiles didn't make their way to Korea until the 17th century). However, once the chile was introduced, it quickly became an important ingredient in most *kimchis*. Today, *kimchi* is often associated with the bright red color of the chile pepper.

During the late months of fall, a lot of Koreans start a process called *Kimjang*, which is when families and neighborhoods get together to create huge batches of *kimchi* to last them through the winter. For *Kimjang*, *Baechu Kimchi* (see page 32) or cabbage *kimchi* is usually made, which is the most common type of *kimchi* and the one used most for cooking (all of the recipes that call for *kimchi* in this book refer back to this one). When cooking *kimchi*, it's really important that the *kimchi* is fermented for at least three weeks so that it's strong, pungent, and full of flavor. If you cook with *kimchi* when it's too young, you're essentially just cooking with cabbage. This means the flavor easily washes away, resulting in watery, tasteless stews and fried rice without any spicy tang. *Kimchi* that has been fermented for several weeks (or even months) is best for soups and stews.

Baechu kimchi can be quite strong and spicy but there are also a lot of other *kimchi* varieties. *Geotjeori* (see page 36) is a *kimchi* that's usually eaten in the spring and summer—it's light and

fresh and can be enjoyed as a salad as a nice contrast to the strong *baechu kimchi* of the winter. Other types include *Dongchimi* (see page 40). This is a water kimchi that doesn't contain any chile flakes, so the liquid is clear and refreshing. As well as seasonal varieties, *kimchi* in Korea differs depending on the region that it's made in. *Kimchi* produced in the northern areas, such as Seoul, are often quite mild, whereas *kimchi* from the warm southern areas are often quite spicy and salty, and contain a lot of fermented fish products due to their proximity to the coast. The *kimchi* recipes in this book are based on the *kimchi* that I've grown up with. My family is from Busan, so these *kimchi* are probably more strongly flavored than those you might have tried before.

While it's pretty easy to buy *kimchi* nowadays, either online or from Asian supermarkets, the ready-made kind will always taste different to the kind you make yourself, not to mention the sense of achievement you'll get from whipping up your own batch. It's possible to "*kimchi*" just about anything, and we wanted to demonstrate this in this book by including some more unusual *kimchi* varieties such as Mango *Kimchi* (see page 38) and Tomato *Kimchi* (see page 41). These *kimchis* are not traditional, but are examples of how the process can be used to ferment almost any firm vegetable or fruit that you might have lying around in your refrigerator at home.

Baechu Kimchi EVERYDAY CABBAGE *KIMCHI*

When I was little, I used to watch my mom make *kimchi*. Standing at the sink, elbow-deep in the *kimchi* "glue," she would rub the mixture into the cabbage before tearing off a little of one of the spicy leaves for me. One was never enough, and I'd always sneak some more until she'd give in and we'd enjoy a pile of the newly made *kimchi* with a steaming bowl of rice. *Kimchi* at this stage is very different from what you might be familiar with since it's fresh and crisp, like a spicy salad, and is deliciously addictive in its own right. If you have the patience to give it a few weeks though, the *kimchi* will develop its characteristic tangy flavor through fermentation, and it is at this stage that it makes a great base for cooking with. No Korean meal is complete without it.

MAKES APPROX.
1³/₄ lb

1¾lb Chinese cabbage, outer leaves and stem removed
3 tablespoons salt

KIMCHI "GLUE"
²/₃ cup *Myeulchi Gookmul* (see page 22)
1 tablespoon sweet rice flour

¼ cup *gochugaru* (Korean red chile powder)
2 scallions, trimmed and finely chopped
1 carrot, finely chopped
4 garlic cloves, minced
½-inch piece of ginger root, peeled and minced

1 apple, finely chopped (skin on)
1½ tablespoons fish sauce
2 teaspoons *saeujeot* (salted fermented shrimp)

1_ Using a sharp knife, make a cut from about 4 inches up the cabbage to the base and use it to gently pull the cabbage in half (this helps to keep the leaves whole without shredding them). Repeat the process with each half so that the cabbage is quartered.

2_ Fill a large bowl with cold water and submerge each of the cabbage quarters fully, then remove from the bowl and shake to get rid of any excess water. Take a small handful of salt and rub it up and down each leaf of 1 cabbage quarter, ensuring the thicker parts closer to the stalk are particularly well covered. Repeat with the remaining quarters, then transfer to a large, clean, resealable plastic container and let stand in the brine for 3 hours, turning the cabbage quarters over every 30 minutes to make sure the salt is distributed evenly over it.

3_ Meanwhile, make the *kimchi* "glue." Bring the stock to the boil in a small saucepan. Add the sweet rice flour, reduce the heat to a simmer, and whisk together until there are no lumps and the mixture is thick enough to easily coat the back of a spoon. Set aside to cool to room temperature, then add the remaining "glue" ingredients and mix together thoroughly (this is easiest done by hand, wearing disposable gloves).

4_ After brining, thoroughly wash the cabbage quarters under cold running water to remove any excess salt or sediment trapped between the leaves, then shake dry. Take a small handful of the "glue" and rub it up and down each leaf of each cabbage quarter to coat,

making sure that the thicker parts nearer the base are particularly well covered, as before. Repeat with the remaining cabbage quarters.

5_ Fold over the top third of each cabbage quarter into its center, then fold over the outer leaves to form a parcel. Pack the *kimchi* parcels tightly into the large container. Spoon any leftover "glue" into the container to fill any gaps. This will help form a barrier against the air and prevent mold from developing. Leave some space at the top of the container because the *kimchi* will need some room to ferment and expand and without this space, it could explode.

6_ Let stand at room temperature for 3 to 4 days to ferment, then transfer to the refrigerator until needed. The *kimchi* will continue to ferment but at a much slower rate, so every day it'll taste a little sharper and a little tangier. Enjoy with everything.

TIP: One way I like to eat really fermented *kimchi* is to wash the seasoning paste off of the leaves, then use these washed leaves to wrap barbecued meats. Or, simply place the washed *kimchi* in one hand, put a small spoonful of rice in the middle with a dollop of *gochujang,* and wrap it up to make a tasty little *kimchi* parcel.

Bok Choy and Radish Kimchi

This is the first non-traditional *kimchi* that Gareth and I ever made. The juicy, crunchy bok choy and radishes make it feel fresh, light, and summery—quite different from the typical cabbage *kimchi*. I once gave a masterclass on how to make different types of *kimchi* and this was by far the most popular. I think people find it less intimidating because it doesn't have the same strong, fermented taste of the more traditional varieties. If *kimchi* is new to you, give this a try.

MAKES APPROX. 3lb 5oz

2¼lb bok choy
9oz radishes, trimmed and halved
1 tablespoon salt
1 tablespoon superfine sugar

KIMCHI "GLUE"
1 cup water
2 tablespoons sweet rice flour
2 tablespoons *gochugaru* (Korean red chile powder)
2 scallions, trimmed and finely chopped
1 carrot, grated
2 tablespoons *saeujeot* (salted fermented shrimp)
1 tablespoon fish sauce
6 garlic cloves, minced
1-inch piece of fresh ginger root, peeled and minced

1_ Using a sharp knife, make a cut about 2 inches long to the base of each bok choy and use it to gently pull the bok choy in half (this helps to keep the leaves whole without shredding them). Repeat the process with each half so that the bok choy are quartered. Rinse the quarters and the radishes under cold running water. Drain, shaking off any excess water, and set aside.

2_ To make the *kimchi* "glue," bring the measurement water to a boil in a small saucepan. Reduce the heat to a simmer, add the sweet rice flour, and beat together until there are no lumps and the mixture is thick enough to easily coat the back of a spoon. Set aside to cool to room temperature, then add the remaining "glue" ingredients and mix together thoroughly.

3_ Meanwhile, mix together the salt and sugar in a bowl. Add the bok choy quarters and rub the salt and sugar mixture between the leaves, ensuring the thicker parts near the base are particularly well covered. Transfer to a large, clean, resealable plastic container along with the radish halves and mix everything together with your hands. Let stand for 30 minutes.

4_ After brining, thoroughly wash the bok choy and radishes under cold running water then shake them dry. Take a small handful of the "glue." Rub it up and down each bok choy quarter to coat, again making sure that the thicker parts nearer the base are particularly well covered. Use the leftover "glue" to coat the radishes.

5_ Fold over the top third of each bok choy quarter into its center, then fold over the outer leaves to form a parcel. Pile the folded bok choy parcels neatly back in the container, filling any gaps with the radish halves.

6_ This *kimchi* can be eaten immediately, but is best after it has had 3 to 4 days at room temperature to ferment, after which you can store it in the refrigerator. It's not great for cooking, so if you want to make a *Kimchi Jjigae* (see page 138) or *Kimchi* Fried Rice (see page 164) you are better off using a traditional *Baechu Kimchi* (see page 32).

Geotjeori QUICK *KIMCHI* SALAD

After a long winter of eating strong fermented *baechu kimchi*, Koreans start to crave something lighter and fresher in spring. *Geotjeori* is a quick *kimchi* that's meant to be enjoyed the day you make it. Crunchy, sweet, and eaten like a salad, it makes a great side to go with barbecued meats and fish.

MAKES APPROX.
1³⁄₄lb

1³⁄₄lb Chinese cabbage, outer leaves and stem removed
2 tablespoons salt
½ medium onion, finely sliced
1 scallion, trimmed and finely sliced
3½ tablespoons *gochugaru* (Korean red chile powder)

3 garlic cloves, minced
½-inch piece of fresh ginger root, peeled and minced
1 tablespoon fish sauce
2 tablespoons superfine sugar

1½ tablespoons sesame seeds
cooked short-grain rice, to serve (see page 26)

1_ Using a sharp knife, make a cut about 2 inches up the cabbage to the base and use it to gently pull the cabbage in half. Repeat the process with each half so that the cabbage is quartered, then repeat again to split the cabbage into eighths.

2_ Cut off and discard the tough base from the bottom of each cabbage section so that it breaks apart into separate leaves. Place the leaves in a large container and sprinkle with the salt, then mix together with your hands to ensure the leaves are completely coated. Let stand for 30 minutes, mixing every 10 minutes to ensure the salt is distributed evenly.

3_ After brining, thoroughly wash the cabbage leaves under cold running water to remove any excess salt, then drain, squeezing out any excess water, and place in a large bowl together with the remaining ingredients. Mix together with your hands thoroughly for 5 minutes, squeezing the leaves as you go—this will release water from the leaves and create a quick sauce. Serve immediately with bowls of rice.

TIP: While this *kimchi* is particularly good eaten the day you make it, you can leave it for a couple of weeks to ferment and enjoy its slightly sweeter flavor in your cooking in the same way as *Baechu Kimchi* (see page 32).

Kkakdugi CRUNCHY TURNIP *KIMCHI*

This super simple *kimchi* is one that my mom would often quickly throw together as I was growing up. *Kkakdugi* is traditionally made from cubed Korean radish (or moo), though back then turnips were much easier to get hold of in the supermarket, and mom would often use these. Mooli, a very similar radish to moo, is easy to find these days in Asian grocery stores and makes a great alternative.

MAKES APPROX. 2lb 11oz

2 tablespoons salt
2 tablespoons superfine sugar
2¾lb turnip, cut into 1-inch cubes

1¼-inch piece of fresh ginger root, peeled and minced
12 garlic cloves, minced
¼ cup *gochugaru* (Korean red chile powder)

2 tablespoons fish sauce

1_ Mix together the salt and sugar in a large plastic resealable container. Add the turnip cubes, toss to coat, and set aside for 1 hour.

2_ After 1 hour, drain the liquid from the turnip cubes. Add the ginger, garlic, *gochugaru*, and fish sauce. Mix everything together well.

3_ Let the *kimchi* stand to ferment at room temperature for 1 week, testing every couple of days to check how strong it tastes, then transfer to the refrigerator and store until needed, when the strength has developed to suit your taste.

Mango Kimchi

While not an obviously Korean ingredient, mangoes really symbolize sunshine for me. I once spent a summer in Jeju Island where some of my family run a mango orchard, and while I was there I was lucky enough to eat the sweet, juicy fruit almost every day. This *kimchi* isn't as strange as it sounds, with the mango bringing a really lovely sweetness to the usually spicy *kimchi* ingredients. It's a great side for a summertime Korean BBQ and goes perfectly with our Pomegranate-glazed Lamb Kebabs (see page 120).

MAKES APPROX.
1lb 2oz

3 x 10½oz unripe mangoes, peeled, seeded, and cut into
   1-inch cubes
2 scallions, trimmed and finely chopped
1 long red chile, coarsely chopped

3 tablespoons fish sauce
2 tablespoons *gochugaru* (Korean red chile powder)
¼-inch piece of fresh ginger root, peeled and minced
2 garlic cloves, minced

1_ Put everything in a large, clean, resealable plastic
container and mix together well to ensure the mango
cubes are evenly coated.

2_ Let the *kimchi* stand to ferment at room temperature
for 3 days before transferring to the refrigerator
until needed.

Dongchimi REFRESHING WATER *KIMCHI*

Unlike most other *kimchi*, *dongchimi* doesn't contain any *gochugaru*, so is a lovely clear, white color. While traditionally made as a winter *kimchi* (when the Korean radishes are in season), it's particularly delicious in summer and its refreshing, cool *kimchi* liquid is often used as a base for chilled noodle soups.

MAKES APPROX.
1³/₄lb

2 tablespoons salt
2 tablespoons superfine sugar
1 mooli, cut into 2 x ¾-inch batons
2-inch piece of fresh ginger root, peeled and thinly sliced
4 whole garlic cloves

1 apple, cut into finger-sized batons
2 scallions, trimmed and cut into thirds
2 long red chiles, trimmed and cut into thirds
4 cups water

1_ Mix together the salt and sugar in a large, clean, resealable plastic container. Add the mooli batons, toss to coat, and set aside for 4 hours, stirring every 30 minutes to ensure the salt and sugar are distributed evenly.

2_ After 4 hours, add the remaining ingredients and mix everything together well. Let the *kimchi* ferment at room temperature for 2 to 3 days before transferring to the refrigerator until needed.

Tomato Kimchi

Because soft fruit and vegetables, such as cucumbers, take on *kimchi* flavors so well, Gareth had it stuck in his head that a tomato version would really work. It turns out he was right. This *kimchi* gets the best out of tomatoes that might not be quite as ripe as you want them to be by intensifying their natural sweetness.

MAKES
2lb 4oz

½ tablespoon salt
½ tablespoon superfine sugar
2¼lb tomatoes, seeded and cut into quarters

1½ tablespoons *gochugaru* (Korean red chile powder)
½-inch piece of fresh ginger root, peeled and minced
3 garlic cloves, minced

1 tablespoon fish sauce
2 scallions, trimmed and finely sliced

1_ Mix together the salt and sugar in a large, clean, resealable plastic container. Add the tomato quarters, toss to coat, and set aside for 30 minutes, mixing again every 10 minutes to ensure the salt and sugar are distributed evenly.

2_ Add the remaining ingredients to the container and, using your hands, mix them together until thoroughly combined.

3_ Leave the *kimchi* to ferment at room temperature for 3 days before transferring to the refrigerator until needed.

03

Banchan & Sides

IF YOU BRUSH

THEM OFF

YOU'LL FIND THAT

EVERYONE HAS

Some Dust

Food is so ingrained in Korean culture that the word for family, shikgu, translates literally as "mouths to feed." Every family gathering always involves a big feast and, whenever we meet with friends, the first thing we talk about is where we should eat.

While Korea's probably best known for its barbecued meats, these are usually reserved for eating out in big groups. At home, people tend to eat an assortment of small dishes known as *banchan*—meat, fish, or vegetable dishes shared in the middle of the table, with each person also having an individual bowl of rice and often a simple soup, or *guk*, as well.

Banchan usually fall into the broad categories of *kimchi* (fermented vegetables), *namul* (lightly seasoned vegetable dishes), *bokkeum* (stir-fried dishes), *jorim* (braised dishes, usually in soy sauce), and *jeon*, which includes savory pancakes (or *pajeon*), but also includes pan-fried meat or vegetables, which are coated in a flour and egg batter. Because Koreans believe that balance is important in order to maintain a healthy diet, there will often be a wide range of different dishes served at any one time.

Nowadays, a lot of (particularly younger) Koreans don't have the time to make a variety of different *banchan* each day, but fortunately they're always easy to buy from the *ajummas* in the markets. Anyone who lives in Korea knows that it is run by the *ajummas*—the middle-aged women often seen wearing baggy floral slacks or track suits and visors. They're the ladies with

attitude—the ones who will shove past you in a street or butt into a line without a second thought. But they're also the powerhouses. It's the *ajummas* who usually run the restaurants, cooking up a storm in the kitchen. They're also the ones with the big trays of food balanced on their head as they deliver takeouts, and the ones who sit for hours at the markets, selling their vegetables and prepared *banchans*.

At work, I used to eat lunch with a group of girls, and we'd always each bring in at least one *banchan*, sometimes homemade, sometimes bought, for everyone to share. These would vary from the traditional, such as homemade *kimchi* or seasoned vegetables to mac 'n' cheese, fried Spam, or wieners tossed in ketchup. It just goes to show that nowadays with *banchan* almost anything goes. It's what I love about Korean food in general—the fact that you're able to pick and choose the dishes you like to suit your own taste.

The dishes that we've included in this section are mostly traditional Korean *banchan*, but they can also be enjoyed as sides or appetizers. We've also included some of our favorite sides, which we've served at our popups and events, all of which would make equally great *banchan* too.

Jeon FAMILY FRITTERS

Though traditionally part of Korea's royal cuisine, nowadays *jeon* can be found everywhere, even as street food. These lightly coated fritters still have a place as part of special occasions, such as *Je-Sah*, which is when families get together to commemorate the lives of relatives who have passed away. In my family we hold a big *Je-Sah* gathering each year to commemorate my grandparents, and these *jeon* always form an important part of the meal we share.

SERVES
4 to **6**

1 tablespoon vegetable oil, plus extra if needed
jeon pieces of your choice (see below)
Cho Ganjang (see page 21), to serve

COATING
4 eggs
1¼ cups all-purpose flour
1 teaspoon salt

1_ Heat the vegetable oil in a large heavy skillet over medium-low heat.

2_ To make the coating, beat the eggs together in a bowl and set aside. In a separate bowl, sift together the flour and salt.

3_ Toss your chosen *jeon* pieces in the flour until well coated, then dip them in the beaten egg mixture.

4_ Shake off any excess beaten egg, then add the *jeon* pieces to the skillet, being careful not to overcrowd it. You may need to cook these in batches. If so, add an extra tablespoon of oil to the pan for each batch.

5_ Fry for 2 to 3 minutes on each side until golden brown, reducing the temperature if it looks like the *jeon* pieces are starting to color too quickly. Remove from the pan and drain on paper towels. Serve with *cho ganjang* for dipping.

Cod (*sengsun*) *Jeon*
Cut ¾lb cod fillet into 2-inch x 1-inch pieces. Coat and cook following the instructions (left).

Zucchini (*hobak*) *Jeon*
Slice 1 zucchini into ½-inch disks. Coat and cook following the instructions (left).

Pork Meatball (*wanja*) *Jeon*
Crumble 7oz firm tofu into a large mixing bowl. Add 1 sliced scallion, 4 minced garlic cloves, 2 tablespoons diced carrot, and 10½oz ground pork, season with salt and pepper, and mix together well. Shape into golf-ball-sized pieces and flatten each until they are about ½ inch thick. Coat and cook following the instructions (left).

Scallion and Spam *Jeon* Skewers (*spam sanjeok*)
Soak 8 bamboo skewers in water. Cut 8 scallions into thirds, then slice 10½oz Spam into pieces of the same size as the onions. Alternately thread 3 scallion and 3 Spam pieces onto each skewer. Neatly trim the skewer ends, then coat and cook following the instructions (left).

HOBAK JEON

SENGSUN JEON

SPAM SANJEOK

Dubu Kimchi STIR-FRIED PORK AND *KIMCHI* WITH TOFU

Don't knock this until you've tried it! While *kimchi* and tofu might not sound like the most exciting of flavor combinations, it really works because the spicy tanginess of the *kimchi* contrasts with the soft, silky texture of the tofu. A great side dish, this is also often served as an *anju* since it makes a perfect accompaniment to a few shots of *soju*.

SERVES
4 to 6
AS A BANCHAN

1 tablespoon vegetable oil
10½oz pork belly, cut into bite-sized chunks
10½oz *Baechu Kimchi* (see page 32), drained and
    coarsely chopped
1 tablespoon *gochugaru* (Korean red chile powder)

1 tablespoon superfine sugar
½ tablespoon roasted sesame seeds
½ tablespoon sesame oil
14oz firm tofu

1_ Heat the vegetable oil in a heavy skillet over medium heat. Add the pork and fry for 2 to 3 minutes, stirring, until the meat is colored on all sides and cooked through.

2_ Add the *kimchi*, *gochugaru,* and sugar to the pan and fry for another 3 minutes, until the *kimchi* softens and becomes glossy from the fat that has rendered down from the pork pieces. Add the sesame seeds and sesame oil and cook, stirring, for another minute, then remove from the heat and set aside.

3_ Bring a saucepan of salted water to a boil. Carefully lower the tofu into the water, reduce to a simmer, and cook for 3 minutes. Remove the tofu from the pan with a slotted spoon and drain on paper towels, then cut into 2-inch squares.

4_ Arrange the tofu squares on a serving plate or board and spoon over the pork and *kimchi* mixture to serve.

Gogi Mandu PORK DUMPLINGS

These plump little dumplings are always a real crowd pleaser. This recipe shows how to make the pan-fried versions with their crispy, golden-brown skins, but they're also great simply steamed or added to soups, and can be deep-fried for added crunch too. I love adding them to instant noodles when I'm feeling really hungry.

MAKES **20** MANDU

vegetable oil, for frying
20 *mandu* skins, either ready-made or homemade (see page 24)
2 tablespoons water, plus extra if needed
Cho Ganjang (see page 21), to serve

FILLING
3 dried shiitake mushrooms
1¾oz *dangmyeon* sweet potato noodles (see page 162)
7oz firm tofu
2 scallions, trimmed and finely sliced
¼ Chinese cabbage, trimmed and finely sliced

3 garlic cloves, minced
pinch of pepper
2 tablespoons regular soy sauce
2 teaspoons sesame oil
1 tablespoon vegetable oil
10½oz ground pork

1_ For the filling, place the shiitake mushrooms in a bowl, cover with boiling water, and let soak for 15 minutes. Drain and finely chop.

2_ Meanwhile, soak the noodles in boiling water in a separate bowl for 10 minutes. Drain and rinse under cold running water, then cut into ¼-inch pieces.

3_ Crumble the tofu into a large bowl (the finer you can crumble it, the better). Add the noodles and mushrooms to the tofu along with all the remaining filling ingredients except the ground pork and mix together well.

4_ Heat 1 tablespoon of vegetable oil in a skillet over medium heat. Add the ground pork, stirring, and break it into pieces with a wooden spoon until browned all over. Add the filling mixture to the pan and cook for another 3 minutes, stirring, until the cabbage has softened. Transfer the filling to a large bowl and let cool.

5_ Fill the *mandu* skins following the step-by-step instructions (right).

6_ Heat 2 tablespoons of oil in a large skillet with a lid over medium heat. Add the *mandu*, being careful not to overcrowd the pan (you may need to do this in batches) and fry for 2 minutes until browned on one side.

7_ Turn the *mandu* over, add the water, and cover with the lid. Cook for 2 minutes, then remove the lid. The *mandu* should be half-crispy and half-steamed at this point. If there's still a little water in the pan, then let them cook, uncovered, for another minute until it has evaporated.

8_ Drain on paper towels and serve with *cho ganjang* for dipping.

MANDU-FILLING STEP-BY-STEP

1_ Lay a *mandu* skin flat in the palm of your hand.

2_ Spoon 2 teaspoons of the filling into the center of the *mandu* skin.

3_ Dab a finger in a little water and run it over the edge of half of the *mandu* skin.

4_ Fold the *mandu* skin over and seal the edges together with your fingertips.

5_ Dab your finger in a little more water and run it over the front flat edge of the *mandu*.

6_ Ensuring the *mandu* skin remains flat, pinch the semicircular side with your fingertips every ½-inch along the edge to create a rippled, crimped effect. Repeat with the remaining *mandu* skins and filling.

Haemul Pajeon CRISPY SEAFOOD PANCAKE

Apparently, Koreans traditionally eat these deliciously crispy savory pancakes on rainy days because the sizzling noises from the skillet sound like the pitter-patter of raindrops. While this seems like a bit of a stretch to me, I'm happy for any excuse! The baking powder is the secret ingredient in this recipe—it gives the pancake extra crunch, so everyone will be fighting over all those crispy edges. It's served traditionally with *makgeolli*, a fermented alcoholic rice drink, but it is also great with a *soju* or beer.

MAKES
2
LARGE
PANCAKES

2 cups all-purpose flour
1 teaspoon salt
1 teaspoon baking powder
13fl oz ice-cold sparkling water

7oz mixed seafood (such as shrimp, mussels, and squid rings), coarsely chopped
2 bird's-eye chiles, finely chopped (optional)
10 scallions, trimmed and cut into 2-inch pieces

⅓ cup vegetable oil, divided, plus extra if needed
Cho Ganjang (see page 21), to serve

1_ In a large bowl, mix the flour, salt, and baking powder together with the water to form a smooth batter. Add the seafood, chiles, and scallions and stir together well to ensure everything is evenly coated in the batter mixture.

2_ Heat half of the vegetable oil in a large, nonstick skillet over high heat. Spoon a generous ladleful of the pancake mixture into the center of the pan then, using the rounded base of the ladle, carefully smooth the mixture out into a circular shape until the pancake is about ½ inch thick.

3_ Cook the pancake for 2 to 3 minutes, until browned and crispy on one side, then flip it over and cook for another 2 to 3 minutes. The pancake will soak up some of the oil, so you may need to add a little extra to stop it from sticking (this will also help to make the edges extra crispy). Drain on paper towels and cover to keep warm.

4_ Heat the remaining oil in the skillet and repeat for the second pancake. Serve with *cho ganjang* for dipping.

Coconut Bindaetteok CRISPY MUNG BEAN PANCAKES

These mung bean pancakes are particularly famous in Gwangjang Market in Seoul, where you can watch as the *ajummas* grind up the mung beans by hand using stone mills, to create the paste for the pancake batter. The batter is then fried in batches on large sizzling griddles and the pancakes are piled high at the front of the *ajummas'* market stands, to catch the eye of passing customers. The fragrance of these *bindaetteok* crisping up in the hot oil fills the market, making them impossible to resist.

We wanted to create our own take on these mung bean pancakes and decided to give them a South-Asian twist for a Korean/Indian popup that we held with some friends. The coconut adds a subtle sweetness, which provides a nice contrast to the tangy, sweet-and-spicy dipping sauce that we serve these with.

MAKES
8
PANCAKES

2¼ cups yellow mung beans
1½ cups coconut milk
3½oz creamed coconut, grated
1 teaspoon salt

1½ teaspoons garam masala
1 onion, finely sliced
2 bird's-eye chiles, finely sliced
vegetable oil, for frying

DIPPING SAUCE
2 bird's-eye chiles, finely sliced
3 tablespoons apple vinegar
2 tablespoons superfine sugar
½ tablespoon *gochugaru* (Korean red chile powder)

1_ Put the mung beans in a bowl, cover with water, and let soak for 4 hours.

2_ Meanwhile, for the dipping sauce, mix all the ingredients together in a bowl. Set aside.

3_ Once soaked, rinse and drain the mung beans, then add them to a food processor with the coconut milk, creamed coconut, salt, and garam masala and blend together to form a smooth batter. Stir the onion and chiles into the batter with a wooden spoon.

4_ Heat 2 tablespoons of vegetable oil in a large skillet over medium heat. Pour a ladleful (about ½ cup) of batter into the pan and spread out to a ½-inch thickness. Fry for 2 minutes on each side until crispy and golden.

5_ Slide the pancake out of the pan and drain on paper towels while you continue to make the rest, adding an extra 2 tablespoons of oil to the pan for each pancake. Serve immediately with the dipping sauce.

Pa-Jeori SCALLION SALAD

My mom is from Busan, so I've always thought that this dish was called *Pa-Jeo-Leg-Gi*. That is, until I was teased about it recently. Korea has different accents and dialects, and this is just one example of the many words from Busan that are creeping into my Korean without me realizing it. The official name that you'll see on restaurant menus is *Pa-Jeori*. However you say it, these spicy scallions make a great accompaniment to a Korean BBQ, the slightly vinegary dressing contrasting perfectly with the fatty meats and sweet marinades.

SERVES
4
AS A BANCHAN

7oz scallions, trimmed
2 tablespoons regular soy sauce
2 garlic cloves, minced
2 tablespoons *gochugaru* (Korean red chile powder)

2 teaspoons sesame oil
2 tablespoons superfine sugar
2 tablespoons apple vinegar
1 teaspoon salt

1_ Cut the scallions into 4-inch pieces, then cut each piece in half lengthwise. Slice the scallion halves lengthwise as thin as you possibly can so that you have lots of fine scallion strands.

2_ Place the scallion strands in a large bowl with all the remaining ingredients. Using your fingertips, mix the ingredients together well for 2 to 3 minutes. When the scallions are softened and completely coated they are ready to serve.

Gyeran Jjim FLUFFY STEAMED EGG

This dish is so simple but so delicious, and is one of my favorite *banchan*. The egg becomes really light and fluffy like a soufflé, lightly seasoned by the fermented shrimp. If you find the idea of seeing the whole little shrimp off-putting, either chop them up before you add them to the egg or use a good pinch of salt instead.

SERVES
4
AS A BANCHAN

3 eggs
approximately 1 cup water
1½ scallions, trimmed and chopped

½ teaspoon vegetable oil
2 teaspoons *saeujeot* (salted fermented shrimp)

1_ Crack the eggs into a large measuring cup, making a note of the volume of egg (this should be about 1 cup but will vary depending on the size of the eggs you use). Top off with the same quantity of water as egg, add half the scallions, and beat together well.

2_ Brush the bottom of a heatproof earthenware dish or Korean *dolsot* stone bowl with the vegetable oil and place over high heat.

3_ Add the egg mixture to the dish and cook for 3 to 4 minutes, beating continuously, until the egg thickens to a consistency like custard. Beat the fermented shrimp into the mixture and cook for another minute, until the egg is just beginning to set and is starting to come away from the sides of the dish.

4_ Remove from the heat, spoon into a serving bowl, and garnish with the remaining scallions. Serve immediately.

A generic term for anything that has been mixed in seasoning, *muchim* are commonplace on a Korean dinner table as *banchan*. These dishes can always be found in our refrigerator at home—my mom will often grab a small handful of each and mix them together with rice and sesame oil to make a very quick *bibimbap* (mixed rice), but they can also be served as individual dishes.

In Korea, there's a phrase, "*son mat*," which means "taste of the hand." It refers to a person's natural ability to balance flavors to create a dish. The *muchim* recipes that feature here are my versions, but everyone makes them slightly differently, so feel free to adjust them to your own taste. Funnily enough, it's actually easiest to mix all of the ingredients together by hand rather than using a spoon, because it means you really rub the flavors into the vegetables and encourage their natural juices to form the marinade.

Sigeumchi Muchim SEASONED SPINACH

▌ Lightly seasoned, the sesame flavorings give the earthy spinach a subtle, nutty fragrance.

SERVES
6
AS A BANCHAN

14oz fresh spinach
½ teaspoon salt
1 small garlic clove, minced

1 teaspoon sesame oil
pinch of pepper
1 tablespoon roasted sesame seeds

1_ Bring a large saucepan of water to a boil.

2_ Add the spinach to the water and cook for 1 minute until wilted. Drain and rinse under cold running water, then squeeze out any excess water with your hands.

3_ Put the spinach in a bowl, add the remaining ingredients, and mix together with your hands, ensuring the spinach is thoroughly coated in the seasoning mixture. This will keep in the refrigerator for 3 to 4 days.

Kongnamul Muchim SEASONED BEAN SPROUTS

▌ An essential for *Dolsot Bibimbap* (see page 167), these beansprouts have a nice crunchy texture and are a staple banchan at most Korean tables.

SERVES
6
AS A BANCHAN

1lb 5oz beansprouts
2 tablespoons salt
4 scallions, trimmed and finely sliced

2 garlic cloves, minced
1 tablespoon roasted sesame seeds
1 tablespoon sesame oil

1_ Remove any brown heads and skins from the bean sprouts and cut off all the stringy roots.

2_ Fill a large saucepan with water and bring to a boil. Reduce the heat to a simmer, add the bean sprouts, and cook for 5 minutes until tender. Drain and rinse under cold running water.

3_ Tip the bean sprouts into a large bowl and add all the remaining ingredients. Mix everything together with your hands, ensuring the bean sprouts are thoroughly coated in the seasoning mixture. This will keep in the refrigerator for 3 to 4 days.

Miyuk Muchim SEASONED SEAWEED

Probably my mom's favorite *muchim*, this seaweed *banchan* still retains the taste of the sea with a very savory edge from the onions.

1oz dried *miyuk* (wakame) seaweed
1 tablespoon vegetable oil
½ onion, finely sliced

pinch of salt
2 teaspoons sesame oil
2 tablespoons sesame seeds

1 teaspoon light soy sauce
1 small garlic clove, minced

1_ Put the seaweed in a small bowl, cover with cold water, and let stand for 10 to 15 minutes until soft and slippery. Drain, squeezing out any excess water with your hands, then coarsely chop.

2_ Heat the oil in a heavy skillet over medium heat. Add the onion and salt and fry for 2 to 3 minutes, until the onion has softened but not colored.

3_ Transfer the onion to a large bowl and add the chopped seaweed, sesame oil, sesame seeds, soy sauce, and garlic. Using your fingertips, mix the ingredients together well, ensuring the seaweed is thoroughly coated in the seasoning mixture. This will keep in the refrigerator for 3 to 4 days.

TIP: If you want something spicier, leave out the onions and soy sauce and mix in a couple of tablespoons of *Cho Gochujang* (see page 18) when combining the rest of the ingredients. This will make a spicy, sweet and sour seaweed *muchim* called *miyuk cho muchim*.

SIGEUMCHI MUCHIM

MIYUK MUCHIM

KONGNAMUL MUCHIM

Corn on the Cob with Kimchi Butter

Oozing with melted butter, corn on the cob has to be one of the ultimate side dishes and the perfect accompaniment to a BBQ. Our *Kimchi* Butter, slathered on top, packs the corn full of salty, spicy flavors. Be generous with it because you'll want loads.

SERVES
8
AS A BANCHAN

4 cobs of corn, husks removed, halved
2 tablespoons vegetable oil
½ teaspoon salt

KIMCHI BUTTER
7oz *Baechu Kimchi* (see page 32), drained
2 sticks butter, softened

2 teaspoons fish sauce
4 garlic cloves, minced
1 tablespoon *gochujang* (Korean red chile paste)

1_ To make the *kimchi* butter, put all the ingredients in a bowl. Mix everything together well with a wooden spoon (or use your hands if you prefer) until the ingredients are incorporated evenly through the butter.

2_ Transfer the butter to a cutting board covered in a sheet of plastic wrap and form into a long sausage shape about 2 inches in diameter. Cover the butter tightly in the plastic wrap, twisting the edges to seal, and refrigerate until needed.

3_ When you are ready to cook the corn, mix the vegetable oil together with the salt in a small bowl.

4_ Heat a cast-iron ridged grill pan over medium heat. Brush the corn with the oil mixture, then add to the pan and cook for 10 to 12 minutes, turning with a pair of tongs and brushing with more oil every few minutes to ensure they cook evenly, until the kernels become swollen and start to make a popping noise.

5_ Stand the cobs of corn upright and cook them for 30 seconds on each end to sear and ensure all the kernels are cooked. Transfer to a large serving dish.

6_ Cut the *kimchi* butter into disks and slather all over the corn to serve.

TIP: Although you'll want to use lots of butter here, any left over will keep in the freezer for up to a month.

Ga-ji Bokkeum STIR-FRIED CHILE EGGPLANT

I love the way eggplant acts like a sponge and soaks up other flavors, and I particularly enjoy them when they're stir-fried. In this dish it's really important to salt and squeeze the eggplant first, so make sure not to skip this step—it will transform the eggplant from the sludgy stuff of nightmares to the beautifully caramelized, slightly sticky pieces you're after here.

SERVES
4
AS A BANCHAN

1 eggplant, trimmed
½ tablespoon salt
1 tablespoon vegetable oil

SAUCE
6 garlic cloves, minced
2 tablespoons *doenjang* (Korean soybean paste)
½ tablespoon liquid honey
½ teaspoon sesame oil
½ tablespoon sesame seeds

pinch of pepper
1 tablespoon regular soy sauce
½ tablespoon mirin
1½ long chiles, trimmed and finely chopped
1 scallion, trimmed and finely chopped

1_ For the sauce, put all the ingredients in a small bowl and mix together well. Set aside.

2_ Slice the eggplant in half lengthwise, then slice each half into quarters so that you end up with eight long strips. Cut each strip into a piece 2¾ inch long.

3_ Put the eggplant pieces in a large bowl and cover with the salt. Let stand for 15 minutes to draw out any excess water. Squeeze the pieces by hand to dry further (it's easiest to do this a few pieces at a time).

4_ Heat the vegetable oil in a skillet over high heat. Add the eggplant pieces and fry, stirring occasionally, for 4 to 5 minutes, until the flesh is softened and caramelized. Reduce the heat to medium, stir in the sauce to coat the eggplant pieces, and fry for another 3 minutes. This will keep in the refrigerator for 3 days.

Gamja (Potato) Salad

Surprisingly, potato salad is one of those dishes that you often find at Korean restaurants, served alongside the *kimchi* as *banchan*. To be honest, it's never been one of my favorite choices since it's usually very heavy on mayonnaise and doesn't tend to have much flavor. This version however, which has smoky bacon, sharp mustard, and tangy sour cream, will have everyone fighting over the last potato.

SERVES
4
AS A BANCHAN

2¼lb new potatoes
1 tablespoon salt
3 slices smoked bacon, finely chopped

2 scallions, trimmed and finely sliced
1 cup sour cream
½ teaspoon English mustard

pinch of pepper
1 small garlic clove, minced

1_ Cut any large potatoes in half so that they are all approximately the same size.

2_ Bring a large saucepan of water to a boil. Add the salt and potatoes, reduce the heat to a simmer, and cook for 10 to 15 minutes, or until the potatoes are tender when pierced with a knife. Drain, rinse under cold running water to cool, then tip into a bowl. Set aside.

3_ Heat a skillet over medium heat. Add the chopped bacon and cook, stirring, for 2 to 3 minutes, until lightly browned and crispy. Remove from the heat.

4_ Add the bacon to the potatoes, making sure to include all the crispy bits sticking to the skillet, along with any rendered fat. Add the remaining ingredients and toss together well until the potatoes are completely coated in the dressing and then let cool. Serve at room temperature.

Myulchi Bokkeum CANDIED ANCHOVIES

You know that saying, "Mother knows best"? Well, in this case, my mom really does. I first tried making a version of this (actually very easy) side dish at home, and the result was slightly burnt, quite bitter, and very salty. So, I called my mom for her recipe and here it is. Her method produces sticky, crispy anchovies with a great chile kick. Traditionally, these anchovies would be served in the middle of the table alongside some *kimchi* and lots of other *banchan*, but Gareth insists that they also make a great beer snack.

SERVES
6 to 8
AS A BANCHAN

1 tablespoon vegetable oil
1¾oz small dried anchovies, about ¾ inch long
2 bird's-eye chiles, trimmed and finely sliced
3 tablespoons regular soy sauce

3 tablespoons corn syrup
1 tablespoon water

1_ Heat the vegetable oil in a heavy skillet over medium heat. Add the dried anchovies and chiles to the pan and fry for 1 minute, stirring to ensure the fish are evenly coated in the oil. Transfer the anchovies and chiles to a plate and set aside.

2_ Return the skillet to the heat and add the soy sauce, corn syrup, and water. Simmer for 1 to 2 minutes, stirring to prevent the liquid from sticking to the bottom of the pan, until it has reduced to a thick, sticky syrup.

3_ Return the anchovies and chiles to the pan and mix together with a wooden spoon to ensure they are evenly coated. Then remove from the heat and spoon into a suitable container. Let cool, then cover and store in the refrigerator for up to a week until needed.

TIP: For a very quick, hassle-free dinner simply mix these anchovies through a little cooked rice.

Ya-che Ssam Moo PICKLED MOOLI PARCELS

I had these tangy little mooli parcels at my cousin's house in Seoul. It was the first time we'd visited her place since she'd got married and she served them as an appetizer, which was very unusual for Korean food! While they might not pack the big punchy flavors of some other Korean dishes (though the mustard dipping sauce gives them a lovely kick) they are beautifully crisp and fresh and make the perfect canapé if you're having a party, or a lovely light appetizer before a heavy meal.

SERVES
8
AS A BANCHAN

4 scallions
20 pickled mooli slices (see Tip)
1 carrot, halved and cut into thin strips
1 red bell pepper, cut into thin strips

1 Boston or Bibb lettuce heart, finely chopped

DIPPING SAUCE
1 teaspoon superfine sugar

1½ teaspoons English mustard or wasabi
1 tablespoon apple vinegar
1 teaspoon regular soy sauce

1_ Slice the green parts of the scallions lengthwise to create long thin strips. Discard the white parts.

2_ Mix all the dipping sauce ingredients together in a small bowl. Set aside.

3_ Arrange a few carrot and bell pepper strips in the center of one mooli slice and top with a small pinch of chopped lettuce.

4_ Roll the mooli into a cigar-shaped parcel, tucking in the vegetables (don't worry if some poke out of the ends). Tie a scallion strip around the middle of your parcel to hold everything in place, then repeat with the rest of your mooli slices and filling ingredients.

5_ Arrange the mooli parcels on a large plate and serve with the dipping sauce.

TIP: Pickled mooli slices can be bought at most Korean supermakets and come in round packages. If you can't get hold of these, you can make your own by shaving a mooli with a vegetable peeler into long, wide ribbons. Cut the ribbons into 4-inch pieces and pickle them using our Simple Pickle Brine recipe (see page 82). Don't feel bound by the choice of vegetable for the filling here either. Just use whatever crunchy vegetables you have handy.

Mooli Slaw

We usually serve this as a topping for our *Jeyuk Bokkeum* (see page 108) pork belly buns. The pork belly is quite spicy, so the fresh and crunchy slaw gives it a cooling, refreshing contrast. If you let this slaw sit, the vegetables will release too much liquid, making it watery, so for best results be sure to serve it immediately after making it.

SERVES
4
AS A BANCHAN

¾lb mooli, coarsely grated
1 carrot, grated
⅓ cup apple vinegar

⅓ cup plain yogurt
pinch of salt

1_ Put the grated mooli in a salad spinner and spin to get rid of any excess liquid. Drain and repeat until the mooli is quite dry.

2_ Put the mooli in a bowl, add the remaining ingredients, and mix together thoroughly. Serve immediately.

YA-CHE SSAM MOO

Pickles & Sauces

ASK
THEN
GO
Even on a road
YOU
KNOW

No one likes dry food. ~~Food should be moist, juicy, and~~ (in Gareth's opinion) covered in plenty of sauce. The Big Mac "special sauce" is what gives the burger its tang and keeps it moist. Some people think so much of it that McDonald's was able to recently auction off a batch of 200 bottles of it for $20,000. While that seems a little crazy, I guess it goes to show how much some people appreciate a good sauce.

Just as the *jang* ingredients in the basics section represent the backbone of Korean cooking, the sauces here represent the backbone of our street-food twist on Korean food.

Ssamjang Mayo

We top our burgers with *Ssamjang* Mayo (see page 83) to give them that salty earthiness that you typically get with *ssamjang* in a barbecue wrap. Mixing it with mayo makes it a little less intense, but it gives the burger an extra depth of flavor and makes a really great dipping sauce for fries.

Sweet Chile Sauce

Our Korean Sweet Chile Sauce (see page 86), or "chicken sauce" as we usually call it on our trailer, is sweet, garlicky, and a touch spicy. It's based on the best fried-chicken sauces we've had in Korea and is just delicious slathered over everything.

Mehwah Jam

The *Mehwah* Jam (see page 85) or "spicy jam" we make is full of fiery heat from the Scotch bonnet chile, but is sticky and sweet too. This combination of sugar and intense heat makes it really addictive, and it goes so well with cheese. Gareth actually made a very similar jam for our wedding, where we had an evening buffet of cured meats, cheeses, and pies—this spicy jam is the perfect accompaniment to anything like this.

Pickle Brine

We love *kimchi*, but it can sometimes be a little too punchy when eaten with certain dishes, which is when we like to use other pickled vegetables instead. These are often eaten in Korea since they are a good way to preserve vegetables. They can be pickled in *gochujang*, in soy sauce, or simply with sugar and vinegar, to create a nice, sharp contrast against any heavier foods. With fried chicken, for example, mooli that's very simply pickled is the perfect accompaniment since it is clean and fresh. We've found that the Pickle Brine (see page 82) that we use for mooli works really well with other vegetables, too. We had to include it here as it gives vegetables a refreshing zing but isn't so overpowering that you can't taste their natural flavors. It's the simplest recipe to remember and is a great one to have up your sleeve.

Onions Pickled with Mustard Sauce

These pickled onions are a popular accompaniment to Korean BBQ, since the tangy vinegar cuts against the (often sweet) marinades and heavy meats. We top our burgers with them for the same reason, and they also make a great side for cold cuts, particularly the *Gochujang* Meatloaf (see page 110). While onions in Korea are very mild and are often eaten raw, regular brown onions can be a little more pungent, so we tend to soak them before pickling to get rid of any harsh flavors.

MAKES 1 SMALL JAR

2 onions, finely sliced
pinch of salt
½ cup English mustard

½ cup superfine sugar
½ cup apple vinegar

1_ Put the onions in a bowl and cover with water. Add the salt and let soak for 10 minutes.

2_ Meanwhile, in a separate large bowl, mix together the mustard, sugar, and apple vinegar.

3_ Once soaked, drain the onions and add them to the mustard sauce. Mix together thoroughly so that the onions are completely coated. Either eat immediately or, for best results, transfer to a small jar and let stand in the refrigerator for 24 hours to soften.

Zingy Green Sauce

This zingy sauce is not very Korean at all. In fact, both limes and cilantro are difficult to get hold of in Korea, yet it works fantastically well with Korean BBQ. One winter, we collaborated with our friends Ben and Aneesha to hold an Indian/Korean night at a local restaurant. We tested lots of different recipe ideas and were surprised to discover all the overlaps between the two cuisines (think chutneys, pickles, and spices), and their Indian green chutney was one of my highlights of the night. This recipe adds a delicious freshness to any dish and makes a perfect partner for our *Kimchi* Salsa (see below) as a dipping sauce.

MAKES APPROX. **13oz**

7oz cilantro, leaves and stalks
2 scallions, trimmed
1 whole garlic clove

½oz fresh ginger root, peeled
½ long chile (optional)
juice of 3½ limes, plus extra if needed

Put the cilantro, scallions, garlic, ginger, and chile, if using, in a food processor. Add the lime juice and blend until smooth, pouring in a little more lime juice if the sauce is looking too thick. Serve or keep refrigerated for up to 3 days.

Kimchi Salsa

Korean-Mexican food is really big in both Korea and the USA. The punchy flavors of both countries really complement each other, while Mexican salsas and sauces lend Korean foods a bright, zesty freshness. This tomato salsa has a subtle Korean tangy kick from the *kimchi*. It's quick and easy to prepare and makes a perfect accompaniment for Korean BBQ, as well as a great dipping sauce for Lotus Root Nachos (see page 215).

MAKES APPROX. **13oz**

2 tomatoes
½ red onion
2 tablespoons matured *Baechu Kimchi* (see page 32)

pinch of salt
2 tablespoons *gochugaru* (Korean red chile powder)
small handful of cilantro leaves, coarsely chopped

Finely chop the tomatoes, red onion, and *kimchi*. Transfer to a serving bowl, add the salt, *gochugaru*, and cilantro leaves, and mix together well. Serve immediately.

Gochujang Ketchup

We had a huge batch of tomatoes in our refrigerator one day, so we decided to use them up by making ketchup. Roasting the tomatoes and charring them a little gives them a nice smoky flavor that works really well with the *gochujang*. It's ketchup—you know what to do.

MAKES APPROX
1lb 7oz

2¼lb tomatoes, halved
1 onion, coarsely chopped
1 teaspoon salt
3 tablespoons vegetable oil, divided

1 long red chile, trimmed and coarsely chopped
6 garlic cloves, minced
3 tablespoons *gochujang* (Korean red chile paste)
½ cup apple vinegar

2 tablespoons regular soy sauce
½ cup soft brown sugar
2 tablespoons *gochugaru* (Korean red chile powder)
3 tablespoons water

1_ Preheat the oven to 350°F.

2_ Put the tomato halves in a large bowl, add the onion, salt, and 2 tablespoons of the vegetable oil and mix together well.

3_ Transfer the tomato mixture to a roasting pan, laying the tomato halves out flat to prevent them from overlapping, and roast in the oven for 40 minutes until the tomatoes are softened and beginning to color at the edges. Remove from the oven and let cool, then transfer to a food processor, add the chile, and blend together until silky smooth.

4_ Heat the remaining vegetable oil in a heavy saucepan over low heat. Add the garlic and fry for 1 minute until softened, then add the blended tomatoes along with all the remaining ingredients. Bring to a simmer, cover, and let cook for 20 minutes.

5_ Strain the ketchup through a sieve, discarding the pulp, and pour into a large clean jar. Store in the refrigerator for up to a week.

Simple Pickle Brine

This simple pickle brine is traditionally used to make the pickled *moo* (Korean radish) cubes that are served at almost every fried-chicken outlet in Korea. We use it a lot on our trailer and for events because it's subtle, clean, and refreshing. Our favorites include apple and chile pickle, pickled mooli cubes, and pickled cauliflower, though it works with pretty much any vegetable.

The recipe works as follows:

1_ Mix together equal parts superfine sugar, water, and apple vinegar, making enough to cover whatever vegetable you plan on pickling.

2_ Put your chosen vegetable in a suitable container, cover with the brine, then let stand in the refrigerator for at least 24 hours.

It's that simple!

Really Great Cheese Sauce

There are so many uses for this cheese sauce. You can top your burgers with it, stir it into cooked pasta, or eat it as a cheese fondue. The choice is yours. The amount of chile powder and garlic used here might be tiny but they make all the difference, their subtle background flavor transforming the sauce from being just something rich and heavy into something truly irresistible.

MAKES APPROX
2¼
cups

½ stick butter
½ cup all-purpose flour
1¾ cups whole milk, plus extra if needed
3½oz medium Cheddar cheese, shredded

3½oz red Leicester cheese, shredded
pinch of extra-hot chile powder
pinch of salt
1 garlic clove, minced

1_ Slowly melt the butter in a saucepan over medium heat (don't rush this because you don't want the butter to color). Add the flour to the butter and stir continuously together to form a smooth paste (roux). Continue to cook, stirring, for 2 to 3 minutes, then gradually add the milk, stirring constantly with a whisk to stop it from sticking to the pan and becoming lumpy.

2_ Stir in the shredded cheeses, then add the remaining ingredients, stirring, and cook for a further 2 to 3 minutes, until all the cheese has melted. If you feel the sauce is getting too thick, stir in another splash of milk to thin it out. This can be made in advance; heat through over medium heat (adding extra milk if necessary) when ready to use.

Ssamjang Mayo

Adding a touch of *ssamjang* to mayonnaise gives it a rounded umami depth that brings out all the meaty flavors of a burger. This slightly salty mayo is also a great dipping sauce for fries, especially when mixed together with *Mehwah* Jam (see page 85).

MAKES APPROX. **1 cup**

1 cup mayonnaise, either ready-made or homemade (see below)

2 teaspoons *Ssamjang* (see page 21)
½ teaspoon sesame oil

Spoon the mayo into a bowl, add the *ssamjang* and sesame oil, and stir to combine. Serve or keep refrigerated for up to 3 days.

Joe's Sauce

Our friend Joe runs Korea's biggest English-speaking food blog and is a fountain of Korean food knowledge. So, when he told me about his award-winning paprika-spiked *gochujang* aïoli sauce we had to give it a try. No surprise, it's delicious—perfect for whenever you'd usually eat aïoli or plain mayo, and so much better than either. I never took down exact quantities though, so Joe, we hope you approve!

MAKES APPROX. **1 cup**

1 cup mayonnaise, either ready-made or homemade (see method)
1 tablespoon smoked paprika
6 garlic cloves, minced
2 tablespoons *gochujang* (Korean red chile paste)

2 tablespoons lemon juice

HOMEMADE MAYO
4 egg yolks
½ teaspoon English mustard

pinch of salt
1 tablespoon apple vinegar
1 cup vegetable oil

1_ To make the mayo, put the egg yolks, mustard, salt, and apple vinegar in a food processor and blend together. With the motor running, pour in the vegetable oil in a thin, stready stream until you have a thick, creamy mayonnaise.

2_ Spoon the mayo into a bowl, add the remaining ingredients, and stir together well. Serve immediately or keep refrigerated for up to 3 days.

Mehwah Jam FIERY SCOTCH BONNET CHILE JAM

Our burgers are quite mildly flavored, so we wanted to offer something that could help them pack an extra punch. Enter our *Mehwah* Jam, made with Scotch bonnet chiles. It's definitely fiery, but it is also sweet and sticky, too. While I like to add it to our burgers (I simply can't resist a chile burger), to be honest, I eat it with just about anything. In fact, my favorite way to eat it is spread over cool, creamy goat cheese on top of crispy crackers. Make a batch of this jam and you'll soon be scouring your cupboards looking for things to eat it with, too.

MAKES APPROX.
1lb

¾lb Scotch bonnet chiles
½ cup superfine sugar
¾ cup soft brown sugar

1 cup apple vinegar
pinch of salt

1_ Wearing disposable gloves, cut the tops off of the chiles, and discard them. Put the chiles in a food processor and blend together for 30 to 40 seconds to form a coarse paste.

2_ Transfer the chile paste to a saucepan, and add the remaining ingredients. Bring to a boil for 15 minutes, uncovered, stirring occasionally, until the liquid has reduced by two-thirds and is thick and jammy in consistency. It's a good idea to have your extractor fan on while you do this because these chiles are potent.

3_ Pour into a sterilized jar and let cool. Store, sealed, in the refrigerator for up to a month.

Korean Sweet Chile Sauce

This is our take on a Korean sweet chile sauce, so you can use it as a table sauce to dip your fries into, or simply enjoy it with just about anything. We call this "chicken sauce" on our trailer, since we pour it all over our Korean Fried Chicken (see page 212) and *Ramyun* Chicken Buns (see page 118).

MAKES ABOUT
4 cups

3 tablespoons vegetable oil
12 garlic cloves, minced
¼ cup tomato ketchup
¼ cup *gochujang* (Korean red chile paste)

½ cup corn syrup
3 tablespoons *gochugaru* (Korean red chile powder)
3 tablespoons apple vinegar

1_ Heat the oil in a large skillet over medium-high heat. Add the garlic and fry for 2 to 3 minutes, until softened. Add the rest of the ingredients and cook for another 5 to 6 minutes, until the sauce starts bubbling at the edges. Remove from the heat.

2_ Let cool, then pour into clean, sterilized bottles. Store in the refrigerator for up to a month.

Maneul Jangajji
GARLIC PICKLED WITH SOY

Pickling vegetables in soy sauce is a popular way to preserve them in Korea. Pickling in soy sauce removes the harsh flavors from the garlic cloves, and instead they become quite sweet and tangy. I love eating this thinly sliced on top of slow-cooked braises, such as *Sogogi Gori Jjim* (see page 143) because the sweetness of the pickled garlic lifts the flavor of the rich meat.

MAKES
1
SMALL JAR

50 whole garlic cloves

FIRST BRINE
2 cups apple vinegar
1 cup water
½ cup salt

SOY BRINE
½ cup regular soy sauce
1 cup First Brine Brine
¾ cup superfine sugar
1 cup water

1_ Combine the First Brine ingredients in a resealable container. Add the garlic, cover, and let stand in the refrigerator for 5 days. (Don't worry if your garlic turns blue at this stage, it is simply reacting with the vinegar and is still safe to eat.)

2_ After 5 days, drain the garlic, reserving 1 cup of the First Brine liquid. Set the garlic aside.

3_ Pour the reserved First Brine into a small saucepan over medium heat. Add the Soy Brine ingredients and simmer for 10 minutes, then pour back into the resealable container. Add the garlic, seal, and refrigerate for 10 days before eating.

05

Korean Meat & BBQ

Even the MOON Wanes WHEN IT'S FULL

As we mentioned earlier, Korean BBQ is rarely eaten at home, but it's still a very important part of Korean culture. There are Korean BBQ restaurants lining almost every street in Seoul, and competition among them is fierce.

Korean BBQ is very much about a shared dining experience and most people will go to eat Korean BBQ in large groups (whether that be with family, friends, or with work colleagues), while a lot of restaurants will turn you away if you want Korean BBQ for one. Meat is chosen collectively by the group since it's shared by the whole table, with most restaurants in Korea specializing in a particular meat or even cut. The meat is either offered plain, seasoned with a little salt, or marinated in either a soy-based sauce (such as *Bulgogi* Sauce, see page 95) or *gochujang*. The meat is then served to the table on a large platter, and then it's down to the youngest in the group (within reason) to be in charge of the grill and make sure that the meat is properly cooked for the rest of the table. This is as a sign of respect, because the person cooking usually has the least chance of getting to eat much meat.

The grill is set in the middle of the table (often with space-age style extractor tubes coming down from the ceiling to get rid of the smoke) and everyone helps themselves once it's cooked, making their own lettuce wraps and filling them with the meat and their other chosen fillings. Nowadays, some "fusion" BBQ restaurants have adopted special grills for the center of the barbecue with reservoirs around the edges for cooking eggs or cheese in the meaty juices. I have to admit, I'm still not used to these quite yet—cheese feels like an unusual addition and I prefer the more authentic restaurants. A lot of our favorite types of Korean BBQ are the simple, unmarinated meats.

Korea has many more cuts of meat than American butchers use, so you might have to ask for help you if you're after a particular Korean cut. Koreans tend to like meats that have a lot of marbling for maximum flavor, and often tend to prefer chewier cuts to the ones we're used to (Gareth calls this "the Korean chew"). Korean people have a saying called *shibnen mat* (literally "chewing flavor"), which refers to the flavor you get from chewing your food because they often like to feel that they're properly chewing on something when they're eating. Pork and beef are the most popular meats when it comes to a Korean BBQ. Chicken and duck, and sometimes also shellfish, are also eaten on occasion, but much more rarely.

BEEF

Beef is very expensive in Korea, and much more so than pork. It's probably for this reason that Korea has so many different cuts of beef—around 120 in total—so that the whole cow can really be appreciated and enjoyed. Some of the most popular cuts include:

Deungshim (Rib Eye)

This juicy cut is a popular choice for the barbecue because it's tender, juicy, and has good marbling. The *deungshim* is sliced very thinly so that it cooks quickly.

Anshim (Tenderloin)

Anshim is an expensive cut of meat, cut from the loin of the cow. This section of the cow's muscles doesn't do a lot of work, so it's very tender and mild in flavor.

Chadolbaegi (Brisket)

Chadolbaegi are wafer-thin slices of beef brisket. They are full of marbling, so tend to cause the flames to flare up from underneath as soon as they hit the grill.

Galbi Sal (Rib Meat)

Galbi sal are thin strips of rib meat and are one of the most popular cuts for Korean BBQ because they're less expensive than the other beef cuts, but still have good flavor.

Galbi (Short Ribs)

Korean beef ribs are cut differently to the ones you'd normally get in the US. They take the middle short ribs and cut through the bone, and then open up the meat, without detaching it, so that there's one long strip of beef attached to a chunk of bone at the end. Often when barbecuing, this chunk of bone is cut using a pair of scissors so that all the meat cooks evenly, and then the rib can be enjoyed later because it has a longer cooking time.

LA *Galbi* (Laterally-cut Beef Ribs)

With LA *galbi* the beef is cut lengthwise through the rib bones to create a long, thin strip of beef with a line of rib bones running along the top.

PORK

Pork is the most popular meat in Korea by a long way since it's much less expensive than beef, and most people prefer the fattier cuts because of their flavor and texture.

Samgyeopsal (Pork Belly)

Samgyeopsal translates as "three-layered meat" (sam means three in Korean), due to the layers of fat. Very thinly sliced, this is the most popular Korean cut, though some people can find it a little too rich.

Ogyeopsal (Pork Belly)

Ogyeopsal translates as "five-layered meat," (o means five in Korean). It's cut from the pork belly, just like samgyeopsal, but this part also includes an extra meaty layer with extra pig skin.

Hangjeongsal (Front Neck)

We tried hanjeongsal for the first time on our most recent trip to Korea and wish that we'd had it sooner. Hanjeongsal is cut from the front part of the neck, has lots of marbling and is incredibly tender and juicy.

Galmegisal (Skirt Meat)

Galmegisal is taken from right under the ribs. In some countries, this part would usually be ground up as sausage meat, discarded, or frozen and sent to Asia, which is such a waste as it's our favorite cut of meat. It could easily be mistaken for beef since it's a dark meat that's rich in flavor and quite lean. Galmegisal should be grilled whole over a charcoal barbecue until just cooked through and still a little pink. At this point it should be cut into bite-sized pieces to finish cooking. Gareth's favorite barbecue place in Seoul suggests dipping each piece into a lemon-mustard dipping sauce followed by a little bit of roasted soybean powder, then wrapping it in a lettuce leaf with some ssamjang and a smoky barbecued mushroom. If you can get hold of some galmegisal, you have to try this. It's so good!

KOREAN BBQ AT HOME

On the occasions that we have Korean BBQ at home, we use a small camp stove that we place in the middle of the table. We then set our table as we would for most other Korean meals, with at least five or six different banchan (which would of course include kimchi), along with a soup or stew (in our house it would be Doenjang Jjigae, see page 141) and an individual bowl of rice for each person. We then lay out a big plate of assorted leaves (lollo rosso, Korean sesame leaves, and butterhead lettuce are popular choices) and put some Ssamjang (see page 21) in the middle of the table, along with some hot chiles and raw garlic cloves. Koreans often eat garlic cloves raw as part of a Korean BBQ, but you can also fashion a little cup out of aluminum foil, fill it with oil, and then gently cook the garlic at the same time as the meat, without risking it burning.

For the barbecue itself, as well as the meat (and garlic), we would often add some other ingredients such as kimchi or mushrooms (usually enoki or king oyster), which take on a really nice, smoky flavor.

When it comes to wrapping and eating, the great thing about the Korean BBQ wrap (called ssam) is that you can really add whatever you like to your leaves. Most people though, would eat it like this:

- Take a lettuce leaf in the palm of your hand (I often like to layer a couple of different types of leaves)
- Add a small spoonful of rice (optional)
- If you're eating unmarinated meat, dip it in a little sesame oil and salt
- If you're eating marinated meat, put this straight on top of the lettuce leaf or rice
- Add a smear of ssamjang
- Add a slice of chile or raw garlic on top (optional)
- Add a small pinch of Pa-Jeori (see page 57) or Onions Pickled with Mustard Sauce (see page 76)
- Wrap the lettuce leaf tightly into as small a parcel as you can make it and pop the whole thing into your mouth.

You have to stuff the food in your mouth, so Korean BBQ certainly doesn't make for the most attractive date food, but it's the best way to taste all the flavors at the same time. There's more to Korean food than just barbecue though, so we've included some other examples in this section. Some are meat dishes that have been inspired by the traditional barbecue marinades, such as our Bulgogi Burger (see page 96) whereas others are just our favorite Korean meat or fish dishes, most of which are placed in the middle of the table for sharing.

Kimchi Brine

This brine can lift a meat dish from good to amazing. It's based on the ingredients we use for *kimchi*, and is packed full of flavor, but it also locks in all of the meat's moisture. The means the end result is super juicy. It's really easy to mix together, and is definitely worth making.

MAKES
4
cups

3 long red chiles, trimmed and halved lengthwise
12 garlic cloves, minced
2-inch piece of fresh ginger root, peeled and
   very finely chopped

1½ tablespoons salt
½ cup fish sauce
4 cups water

Mix all the ingredients together in a large bowl.

Bulgogi Sauce

Bulgogi sauce is traditionally used to marinate beef for a Korean BBQ because it really brings out the deep, meaty flavors. Traditional *bulgogi* sauce recipes usually include Asian pears (or sometimes other fruits), which sweeten the sauce and help tenderize the meat. We use apple juice here to create the same fruity flavors but make a nice clear sauce, which we use for our burgers and Philly cheesesteaks.

MAKES ENOUGH FOR
2¼lb
OF BEEF

¾ cup regular soy sauce
½ cup superfine sugar
6 garlic cloves, minced

¾-inch piece of fresh ginger root, peeled and minced
1 tablespoon sesame oil
3 scallions, trimmed and thinly sliced

1 cup clear apple juice

Mix all the ingredients together in a large bowl.

> **TIP:** If you're using this marinade for traditional Korean BBQ, use thin slices of blade steak or sirloin. Marinate the beef for at least 30 minutes before cooking and then grill over high heat for 3 to 4 minutes, or until cooked to your liking.

Bulgogi Burger

Our *bulgogi* burger is one of the bestsellers on our menu and is where it all started for us on our truck. When we first started testing this burger, we quickly found that the traditional *bulgogi* sauce was too thin to stick to the burger patty, making it difficult to taste the flavor of the sauce. After a lot of experimenting, we found that adding a tiny bit of xanthan gum did the trick. A natural binding agent, xanthan gum doesn't have any flavor, but acts to thicken the sauce. If you can't find any, however, use a little cornstarch mixed with water instead.

MAKES
4
BURGERS

1lb 5oz ground beef (ideally coarse-ground, with 20 percent fat)
pinch of salt
1 tablespoon vegetable oil

2 cups *Bulgogi* Sauce (see page 95)
½ tablespoon xanthan gum
4 hamburger buns

TO ASSEMBLE
¼ cup shredded iceberg lettuce
¼ cup Onions Pickled with Mustard Sauce (see page 76)
½ cup *Ssamjang* Mayo (see page 83)

1_ Divide the ground beef into 4 even-sized portions. Being careful not to overwork the beef (otherwise the burgers will become dry), shape the pieces into circular patties around ⅝ inch thick. Season both sides of each patty with the salt.

2_ Heat the vegetable oil in a large heavy skillet over medium heat. Add the burger patties and cook for 2 to 3 minutes on one side without moving or flipping them (you want to build a good crust on it for great flavor and texture). Flip the burger over and cook for another 2 minutes on the other side, again without moving it around the pan.

3_ Put the *bulgogi* sauce and the xanthan gum into a small saucepan and beat the xantham gum vigorously into the sauce. Continue beating for 3 to 4 minutes until the sauce thickens then set to one side.

4_ Put the saucepan over medium heat and keep stirring until the sauce thickens. Be careful not to let it boil otherwise the xanthan gum becomes gloopy.

5_ Slice the buns in half and lay them cut-side down in a large dry skillet over high heat, for 30 to 40 seconds, until warmed through and slightly charred at the edges.

6_ To assemble a burger, arrange some shredded lettuce on the cut side of the bottom half of a bun. Dip a cooked pattie into the warmed *bulgogi* sauce, then place carefully on top of the lettuce. Pour over an extra tablespoon of the sauce (to make things really juicy), and top with a tablespoon of the pickled onions. Smear some mayo on the cut side of the top half of the bun and set on top of the burger to finish. Enjoy with plenty of napkins!

4

Bulgogi Philly Cheesesteak

We cooked these cheesesteaks at our very first popup on a cold night back in February 2014. At the time we thought they were great, but looking back we had never cooked so many dishes in such a short space of time, so we probably didn't do them justice. Since then, we've been working hard to perfect the recipe and we think this is it—the *bulgogi* sauce helps bring out the beefy taste of the meat, and the cheese sauce is finger-licking great. It's really important to use a chewy bread made from potato or rice flour here because the sandwich has so much sauce that anything soft like a brioche bun will just fall apart (and be too sweet), while a baguette has too much crust. Great bread makes a great sandwich and you'll want something to soak up all that meaty juice.

SERVES 4

2½ tablespoons vegetable oil
1½ to 2 tablespoons butter
1 onion, finely sliced
1 red bell pepper, cored, seeded, and finely sliced
⅔ cup *Bulgogi* Sauce (see page 95)

4 x 3½oz sirloin steaks, each about ½ inch thick
4 potato or rice flour buns, each about 4 inches long, halved lengthwise, but not all the way through
1 cup Really Great Cheese Sauce (see page 82)
salt

TO GARNISH
2 scallions, trimmed and thinly sliced
1 tablespoon *gochugaru* (Korean red chile powder)

1_ Heat the oil and butter in a large skillet over low heat. Add the onion, season with a pinch of salt, and fry for 10 minutes, until the onion is silky soft and caramelized. (Be patient—great onions take time.) Add the bell pepper and cook for 3 minutes until slightly softened, then transfer the mixture from the pan to a plate and set aside.

2_ Gently heat the *bulgogi* sauce in a small saucepan over medium heat, being careful not to let it boil because that can make the sauce taste bitter. Meanwhile, heat the cheese sauce in a separate small saucepan over medium heat, adding a little extra milk if it needs thinning. Set both aside.

3_ Place the skillet over very high heat until smoking. Add the steaks and cook for about 40 seconds on each side until done to your liking (you may need to do this in batches). Remove from the pan and let rest for 1 minute.

4_ While the steaks are resting, warm the buns by placing them, cut-side down, in the skillet and heating them through for 30 seconds. Transfer them to plates, cut-side up, and spread the onion and bell pepper mixture evenly over each half.

5_ Cut the steaks into ¼-inch thick strips, add them to the saucepan with the *bulgogi* sauce, and stir to coat evenly. Place the beef strips onto the buns then spoon over the cheese sauce. Serve scattered with scallion slices and sprinkled with the *gochugaru* to garnish.

Yukhoe KOREAN STEAK TARTARE

Though we might be a little biased, this is definitely our favorite way of eating raw beef. Basically a Korean steak tartare, *yukhoe* is made from raw tenderloin or fillet steak that has been lightly marinated to become soft and tender. Flavored with soy and sesame, this dish is very delicate, with the egg yolk acting as a sauce that binds everything together and the lovely balance of sweet and salty really bringing out the beef's natural flavors.

SERVES
2
AS A SHARING
DISH

7oz beef fillet or tenderloin
¼ Asian pear, peeled, cored, and cut into
 fine matchsticks
1 egg yolk
½ teaspoon sesame seeds

½ teaspoon scallion, trimmed and finely sliced

MARINADE
1 tablespoon regular soy sauce
½ tablespoon sesame oil
1 tablespoon roasted sesame seeds

½ tablespoon liquid honey
1 garlic clove, minced
½ scallion, trimmed and finely sliced
pinch of salt

1_ For the marinade, mix together all the ingredients in a bowl. Set aside.

2_ Trim the beef fillet of any fat or sinew and cut it into wafer-thin slices using a sharp knife.

3_ Add the beef slices to the marinade bowl and mix them around with your fingertips to make sure they are completely coated. Add the pear and mix together.

4_ Place a large cookie cutter or chef's ring onto the center of a plate. Spoon the beef mixture into the cutter or ring, pressing down on the edges. Carefully place the egg yolk in the middle.

5_ Remove the cutter or ring and serve scattered with the sesame seeds and scallion slices.

LA Galbi KOREAN-STYLE SHORT RIBS

There's some contention as to where the "LA" in "LA *Galbi*" comes from. Some say that it's proof that the dish originated among the Korean-American population of Los Angeles, while others say it comes from the word "lateral," because of the way the ribs are cut. Whichever is true, this dish is a popular choice for Korean BBQ and it's one we ate a lot as I was growing up.

SERVES 4

3lb 5oz beef ribs, cut into LA *galbi*-style strips (see Tip)
1 tablespoon vegetable oil

MARINADE
2 scallions, trimmed and finely chopped
½ Asian pear, peeled, cored, and finely chopped

½ onion, finely chopped
12 garlic cloves, minced
2-inch piece of fresh ginger root, peeled and minced
pinch of pepper
1 cup regular soy sauce

2 tablespoons sesame oil
3 tablespoons soft brown sugar

1_ For the marinade, mix together all the ingredients in a bowl.

2_ Place the beef rib strips in a large dish. Pour the marinade evenly over the ribs and mix together to ensure the ribs are thoroughly coated. Cover with plastic wrap, transfer to the refrigerator, and let marinate for at least 4 hours, preferably overnight.

3_ When you are ready to cook, heat a ridged cast-iron grill pan over medium-high heat and brush it with the vegetable oil.

4_ Using a pair of tongs, lift the strips of beef out of the marinade, shaking off any excess. Lay the strips flat on the grill pan and cook for 2 to 3 minutes on each side until slightly charred (you may need to do this in batches).

5_ Remove the rib strips from the pan and let cool slightly. Cut the strips at every second bone into smaller pieces to make them easier to pick up and eat.

TIP: For LA *galbi*-style ribs, ask your butcher to cut them thinly across the bone. This will give you long strips of beef with small disks of bone at the top. You can use these bones later as little handles to pick the *galbi* up and eat them by hand.

Donkasu CRISPY PORK SCALLOPS

There are many overlaps between Korean and Japanese cooking, and *donkasu* is just one example. Coming from the Japanese word *tonkatsu*, this hot, crispy, breaded pork scallop is served with a sticky brown sauce that tastes and looks a little like a thicker version of Worcestershire sauce. Traditionally a dish reserved for western restaurants, though now found in restaurants across Korea, the first time I tried it was during a summer in Jeju when I lived with my cousin Jisoo. She was about 12 at the time, and I remember her making me this dish for breakfast one morning. Admittedly, I was a little worried that she'd burn herself on the hot oil, or that the pork wouldn't be cooked through (it was the first time I'd ever seen her cook anything) but the *donkasu* she made was perfectly crispy and delicious and I remember her smiling with pride as she served it up. I've never seen Jisoo cook anything since, so she's either secretly a great cook, or this dish really is just that easy!

SERVES 2

2 x 5½oz pork scallops
1 egg, beaten
⅓ cup all-purpose flour
⅓ cup panko bread crumbs
pinch of salt
pinch of ground white pepper

1 cup vegetable oil

SAUCE
3 tablespoons tomato ketchup
2 tablespoons superfine sugar
1 tablespoon apple vinegar
2 tablespoons regular soy sauce

2 garlic cloves, minced
½ apple, puréed

TO SERVE
¼ white cabbage, shredded
1 cup cooked short-grain rice (see page 26)

1_ For the sauce, put all the ingredients in a saucepan over medium heat, bring to a simmer, and cook, stirring occasionally, for 5 to 6 minutes until the sauce has thickened and easily coats the back of a wooden spoon. Remove from the heat and set aside.

2_ Using a rolling pin, pound the pork escalopes until they are about ½ inch thick.

3_ Pour the beaten egg onto a large plate. Put the flour on a separate plate, smoothing it flat, then do the same with the bread crumbs on a third plate.

4_ Season the pork scallops on both sides with the salt and pepper. Take a scallop and dip it in the flour, then turn over to coat both sides. Shake off any excess flour, then repeat the process with the beaten egg and, lastly, the bread crumbs, pressing the crumbs into the scallop with your fingertips to ensure they stick to the meat. Repeat with the second scallop.

5_ Heat the oil in a large skillet over medium heat to the point where a few bread crumbs dropped into the pan will cause the oil to start to bubble. Gently lay the pork scallops into the skillet (to avoid overcrowding the pan you may need to do this in batches) and fry for 6 to 8 minutes, turning carefully halfway through cooking, until golden brown all over. Carefully remove the scallops from the pan, transfer to a plate lined with paper towels to soak up any excess oil and let cool for 2 minutes.

6_ To serve, gently heat the sauce and spoon the rice into bowls. Cut the scallops diagonally into ½-inch pieces, pushing the knife directly down on top of the pork scallop, rather than sliding it back and forth, to avoid dislodging any of the crispy bread crumbs, then set the pieces onto the cooked rice. Pour over the sauce and accompany with the shredded cabbage.

TIP: Panko bread crumbs can be found in most Asian supermarkets or easily online. If you can't get hold of them, you can use regular dried bread crumbs instead, though you won't get quite the same crunch.

Sticky, Spicy Pork Ribs

These ribs are a tender, juicy, joy to eat. In fact, they're so good, we've even managed to convince our friends to help us move house on the promise of payment with them a couple of times. If you want to use these ribs as a new form of currency like this, just boil them up and pop them in a sturdy resealable plastic bag full of the sauce the night before, then finish them in your new oven as you kick back and enjoy a well deserved beer the following day.

SERVES 6

1lb 2oz pork spare ribs
½ cup coarsely chopped fresh ginger root
5 whole garlic cloves, peeled
½ cup light soy sauce
2 scallions, trimmed and finely chopped, to garnish

SAUCE
1 tablespoon sesame oil
¼ cup *gochujang* (Korean red chile paste)
¼ cup apricot jam
1 tablespoon regular soy sauce
1 tablespoon honey

1 tablespoon roasted sesame seeds
1 tablespoon white rice vinegar
8 garlic cloves, minced
2-inch piece of fresh ginger root, peeled and minced

1_ Put the ribs in a large saucepan or stockpot with the ginger, garlic, soy sauce, and enough water to cover. Bring to a boil, reduce the heat to a simmer, and let cook gently for 1½ hours, until the ribs are tender and cooked through.

2_ Meanwhile, combine all the sauce ingredients in a bowl and mix together well. Line a roasting pan with foil (this will make everything a lot easier to clean up later) and preheat the oven to 400°F.

3_ Arrange the cooked ribs on the prepared pan and brush with the sauce to coat evenly. Roast in the oven for 20 minutes, turning and basting the ribs with more sauce halfway through cooking.

4_ Remove the pan from the oven and put the broiler on high. Brush the ribs once again with the remaining sauce, then broil for 2 to 3 minutes, or until the sauce is sticky and just beginning to char at the edges. Scatter with the scallions and serve.

Jeyuk Bokkeum SWEET AND SPICY PORK BELLY BUNS

We sell this classic Korean spicy stir-fried pork dish on our trailer but make a few small changes to turn it into street food. Firstly we cut the pork much finer, into thin matchsticks, so that the fat melts away and it's easier to eat from a bread bun. We also remove the vegetables, so that the bun is all about the pork, and then we top each bun with a good handful of Mooli Slaw (see page 70).

SERVES
6

2¼lb pork belly, cut into ½-inch slices
1 tablespoon vegetable oil
1 carrot, thinly sliced
¼ white cabbage, thinly sliced
½ onion, thinly sliced

MARINADE
10oz *gochujang* (Korean red chile paste)
6 garlic cloves, minced
½-inch piece of fresh ginger root, peeled and minced
4 teaspoons sesame oil

1⅓ cups superfine sugar
⅓ cup regular soy sauce

TO SERVE
6 white hamburger buns, halved

1_ For the marinade, mix together the *gochujang*, garlic, ginger, sesame oil, and sugar in a large bowl. Stir in the soy sauce to loosen and thin the mixture out.

2_ Cut the pork belly slices into pieces approximately 4 inches long.

3_ Add the pork pieces to the marinade bowl and mix together with your hands to ensure they are evenly coated in the marinade (it may be easiest to do this a little at a time).

4_ Heat the vegetable oil in a large skillet over high heat, add the carrot, cabbage, and onion and cook, stirring, for 3 to 4 minutes until softened. Reduce the heat to medium, then add the pork and marinade mixture to the pan. Cook, stirring continuously to prevent the marinade from sticking to the bottom of the pan, for 15 to 20 minutes or until the pork is cooked through. Divide the pork among the hamburger buns and serve immediately.

Twice-Cooked Crispy Pork Belly

This recipe is arguably the ultimate way to roast pork—think juicy, tender meat, lightly flavored with *doenjang* and honey, alongside loads of crispy, crunchy crackling. It works brilliantly eaten wrapped inside a lettuce leaf, Korean-style, or (Gareth's favorite) piled on top of creamy mashed potatoes with lots of Zingy Green Sauce (see page 79). Whichever way you choose, it's a real crowd pleaser.

SERVES **4 to 6**

2¼lb piece of pork belly
1 tablespoon vegetable oil
1 tablespoon salt

STOCK
1½ cups coarsely sliced fresh ginger root
10 whole garlic cloves

2 tablespoons light soy sauce
2 tablespoons *doenjang* (Korean soybean paste)
2 long red chiles, trimmed and sliced in half lengthwise
1 onion
1 tablespoon black peppercorns

MARINADE
1½ tablespoons *doenjang* (Korean soybean paste)
8 garlic cloves, minced
½-inch piece of fresh ginger root, peeled and minced
1½ tablespoons honey
1 tablespoon apple vinegar

1_ Put the pork belly in a large heavy saucepan or stockpot with all the stock ingredients and enough water to cover. Bring to a boil. Let simmer for 30 minutes, then remove the pork from the stock and let drain. Pat dry thoroughly with paper towels.

2_ Using the tip of a sharp knife, score the skin of the pork belly in a criss-cross pattern, being careful not to cut through to the meat. Transfer to the refrigerator and leave for 4 to 6 hours or preferably overnight to rest.

3_ When ready to cook, preheat the oven to 425°F.

4_ Mix together the marinade ingredients in a small bowl. Place the pork belly skin-side up on a large sheet of aluminum foil and, using a pastry brush, coat the sides and the bottom of the meat only with marinade (be careful not to get any on the skin because it burns easily). Mix the vegetable oil and salt together in a small bowl and brush over the skin.

5_ Fold the aluminum foil around the pork belly to cover the marinated sides, leaving the skin uncovered. Place in the oven on the highest shelf and roast for 30 minutes, then reduce the heat to 350°F and roast for another 30 minutes.

6_ To make really crispy crackling, the pork needs a final blast of heat, so turn the temperature back up to 425°F and cook for 40 minutes more, until the skin is golden brown and crunchy all the way through.

7_ Remove the pork from the oven and let rest for 30 minutes before serving.

Gochujang Meatloaf

I'm a little ashamed to admit that the first time we made this meatloaf, I ate it almost in its entirety, all by myself. It's one of those dishes that is incredibly versatile and can be enjoyed either hot or cold, while the mixture also makes great meatballs or sausages, too. My favorite way to eat it is straight out of the refrigerator, cut into thick slices with a pile of our Onions Pickled with Mustard Sauce (see page 76), though it is also great seared quickly in a skillet for crispy edges, then eaten in a bun with a runny fried egg. Make it on a weekend and you've got breakfast, lunch, and dinner sorted out for the next few days.

SERVES 6

1lb 2oz ground pork
3 scallions, trimmed and finely chopped
6 garlic cloves, minced
1 teaspoon salt
1½ tablespoons *gochujang* (Korean red chile paste)
pinch of pepper

1 cup fresh bread crumbs
½ onion, finely chopped
1 egg

GLAZE
1½ tablespoons apricot jam

1 tablespoon *gochujang* (Korean red chile paste)
½ tablespoon honey
1 teaspoon regular soy sauce
1 garlic clove, minced
¼ teaspoon sesame oil
½ tablespoon apple vinegar

1_ Preheat the oven to 350°F. Grease an 8½ x 4½-inch loaf pan.

2_ For the glaze, mix together all the ingredients in a small bowl. Set aside.

3_ Put all the meatloaf ingredients into a large bowl, then stir together with a wooden spoon until well combined. Add the meatloaf mixture to the loaf pan, pressing it down into the corners and using a knife to level the top smooth. Bake for 45 minutes, or until the meatloaf starts to shrink from the edges of the pan.

4_ Remove the meatloaf from the oven and, using a skewer, poke holes all over the top. Pour the glaze evenly over the top (this will sink into and flavor the meat, as well as forming a lovely topping) and put it back in the oven for another 20 minutes, until the glaze becomes nice and sticky. Serve hot or cold. This will keep in the fridge, covered, for 3 days.

Kimchi Wang Mandu — *KIMCHI* AND PORK STEAMED BUNS

There's something a little magical about watching steamed buns being made in the market—it's the way that they're hidden from sight until they're just cooked, and then revealed in clouds of billowing steam as the lids are lifted from the steamers. These buns can be filled with anything, sweet or savory, although *kimchi* and pork has always been my favorite choice because the salty, spicy filling provides the perfect contrast to the plain, soft, pillowy buns.

MAKES 8 BUNS

vegetable oil, for greasing

DOUGH
1 cup warm water
2½ teaspoons dry active yeast
3 tablespoons superfine sugar, divided
3¾ cups all-purpose flour
1½ teaspoons baking powder

FILLING
1½oz dangmyeon sweet potato noodles
1 tablespoon vegetable oil
10½oz ground pork
pinch of salt
pinch of pepper
5½oz matured *Baechu Kimchi* (see page 32), drained and finely chopped

1 garlic clove, minced
2 scallions, trimmed and finely chopped
1 long red chile, trimmed and finely chopped
1 tablespoon regular soy sauce
6oz firm tofu

1_ To make the dough, in a small bowl, stir together the water, yeast, and 1 tablespoon of the sugar. Set aside for 10 minutes to allow the yeast to activate.

2_ In a large bowl, mix together the flour, baking powder, salt, and remaining 2 tablespoons of sugar. Slowly add the yeast mixture to the bowl and stir together with a wooden spoon to form a dough.

3_ Tip the dough out onto a lightly floured surface and knead for 10 minutes until smooth and elastic. Brush the inside of a mixing bowl with oil and add the dough. Brush the dough lightly with oil, cover loosely with plastic wrap, and let stand in a warm place for 1 hour to prove until doubled in size.

4_ While the dough is proving, make the filling. Soak the sweet potato noodles in enough boiling water to cover for 10 minutes. Drain and rinse under cold water to cool, then cut into ¼-inch pieces. Heat the vegetable oil in a large skillet over medium-high heat, add the ground pork, and fry for 2 to 3 minutes, stirring occasionally, until browned all over. Add the salt, pepper, *kimchi*, and garlic to the pan, cook for 2 minutes more, then add the scallions, chile, and soy sauce. Crumble the tofu evenly over the top and cook for another 2 minutes, using the back of a wooden spoon to break up any large lumps of tofu, then add the sweet potato noodles and mix everything together well. Set aside to cool.

5_ Once it has proved, transfer the risen dough to a lightly floured surface and knead for 5 minutes to punch down any air bubbles. Brush the inside of the bowl with some more oil and return the dough to the bowl, then brush the top of the dough with a little more oil and cover it again loosely with plastic wrap. Let stand to prove for 15 minutes.

6_ Once the dough has proved for the second time, transfer it back onto the floured surface and knead for 5 minutes to loosen it up again. Shape the dough into a long sausage, then divide it into eight equal-sized pieces. Roll each piece out into a thin disk about 4½ inches in diameter.

7_ Flour your hands and take a piece of dough so it lies flat across your palm. Place 2 to 3 tablespoons of the cooled filling into the middle of the dough, then pull one edge of the dough to the center and brush the outside edge with water. Continue pulling the edges of the dough into the center, working around the bun, dabbing it with a little more water each time to stick the dough down. Once all the edges are at the center, twist the middle of the bun to seal.

8_ Cut a sheet of nonstick parchment paper into eight 2¾-inch squares and brush each with a little vegetable oil. Lay these in the bottom of a bamboo or metal steamer, then place a bun (seal-side up) on top of each square, ensuring there is plenty of room between them to allow for expansion while cooking. Steam for 15 minutes, then turn off the heat, remove the lid, and let stand for 5 minutes to allow the excess steam to dissipate.

Serve with *Cho Ganjang* (see page 21) for dipping.

113

O-ri Bulgogi SPICY SHARING DUCK WITH FRIED RICE

This dish will always be pretty special to us. We were introduced to it on Gareth's first trip to Busan by my uncle. We were in a restaurant, sitting on the floor at a low table with the duck simmering in a huge dish in the middle. My family is kind of loud when we all get together, so Gareth was just sitting there eating, taking in the cacophony around him, when all of sudden and much to his surprise, his bowl of rice was whisked away from him. In fact, all the rice from the bowls around the table was collected and thrown into the remaining duck sauce, along with a handful of dried seaweed. The little bits of leftover duck, the sauce, rice, and seaweed were all fried together until the rice began to stick and become a little crispy, before being served back in the original rice bowls. This is the best part of this dish—the rice soaks up all the flavors from the duck and also gets a slightly smoky flavor, as the sauce begins to stick. It'll be the best fried rice you'll ever have, and it's the reason that *O-ri Bulgogi* became Gareth's favorite Korean dish.

SERVES 4

1lb skin-on duck breast, cut into slices ¼ inch thick
1 onion, finely sliced
1 tablespoon vegetable oil
1oz chives, trimmed
1 cup cooked short-grain rice (see page 26), plus extra to serve
1 tablespoon sesame oil

2 dried *gim* (nori) seaweed sheets, sliced into fine matchsticks
2 scallions, trimmed and finely sliced

MARINADE
12 garlic cloves, minced
3 tablespoons *gochujang* (Korean red chile paste)
1 tablespoon *gochugaru* (Korean red chile powder)
2 tablespoons apricot jam or *maesil* (Korean plum extract)
3 tablespoons regular soy sauce
1 teaspoon sesame oil

1_ Mix the marinade ingredients together in a large bowl. Add the duck slices and onion to the bowl and mix together well so that everything is evenly coated in the marinade. Cover with plastic wrap, transfer to the refrigerator, and let marinate for at least 2 hours, preferably overnight.

2_ When you are ready to cook, pour the vegetable oil into a heavy skillet over medium heat. Add the marinated duck mixture to the pan and fry for 4 minutes, stirring and turning the duck pieces as you go, until the duck is just cooked through and the sauce has reduced slightly and become sticky. Stir through the chives until just wilted, then transfer the still-sizzling pan to a heatproof stand in the middle of the table. Serve with rice.

3_ Once you have worked your way through most of the duck and are left with the sticky remains of the sauce and just a few small pieces in the pan, return it to the stove over medium heat. Add the rice, sesame oil, seaweed, and scallions, stir everything together well, then press the mixture against the bottom of the pan with the back of a wooden spoon to create an even layer. Leave for 2 to 3 minutes to get crisp (and to stick a little) on the bottom, then return the pan to the table and enjoy.

Sticky Ginger Roast Chicken

When I think of this roast chicken, I always picture it as a real weekend treat, but it's so simple you could really just as easily have it as a mid-week dinner. Just remember to marinate it and leave it in the refrigerator the night before to keep things quick. You'll be rewarded with super-juicy chicken, slippery sweet onions, and a spicy ginger sauce. All you'll need to finish it will be a simple bowl of steamed rice or vegetables. Workdays can feel long, so it's nice to know you'll have something delicious for dinner, just waiting to be popped in the oven when you get home.

SERVES 4

2 onions
1 whole chicken, about 3lb 5oz
½ cup coarsely sliced fresh ginger root
4 whole garlic cloves
2 scallions, trimmed and cut into thirds

MARINADE
⅓ cup *gochujang* (Korean red chile paste)
½-inch piece of fresh ginger root, peeled and minced
6 garlic cloves, minced
⅔ cup ginger beer

2 tablespoons liquid honey
2 tablespoons light soy sauce
½ tablespoon salt

1_ Combine all the marinade ingredients in a small bowl. Cut the onions into ½-inch slices and arrange them on the bottom of a roasting pan.

2_ Loosely stuff the cavity of the chicken with the ginger slices, garlic cloves, and scallions. Place the chicken in a large bowl or deep tray and pour half of the marinade all over it to cover, making sure to rub it into the creases of the wings and legs as well as the underside. Then place the chicken into the roasting pan with the onions and transfer to the refrigerator to marinate for at least 1 hour.

3_ When you are ready to cook, preheat the oven to 375°F. Place the chicken in the pan on the middle rack and roast for 1¼ hours, brushing it with a little of the remaining marinade every 10 minutes or so.

4_ Remove the chicken from the oven and pour any leftover marinade evenly over it. Turn the oven up to 425°F, return the chicken to the oven, and roast for a further 10 to 15 minutes, until the skin is nicely golden and sticky and the chicken is cooked through. If it looks like it might be getting a littlr too brown at any point, cover it loosely with aluminum foil and continue cooking.

5_ Let the chicken rest for half an hour before carving. Serve with the onions, drizzling a little of the sweet juices from the bottom of the roasting pan over each portion.

Ramyun Chicken Buns

Using instant noodles here to create a coating for the fried chicken not only gives these buns extra crunch, it also helps to lock in all that moisture. The result is really juicy, crispy chicken that's the perfect contrast to a soft bread bun. I've eaten the *Shin* brand of *Ramyun* instant noodles, which is known for being pretty spicy, for as long as I can remember. A few Koreans I know call the little sachet of spice mix they come with "magic dust," and add it to other dishes when cooking for an extra kick. If you're a chile lover, sprinkle a little of it over the cooked chicken thighs for extra heat when serving.

SERVES 6

6 boneless, skinless chicken thighs
4 cups *Kimchi* Brine (see page 94)
2 x 4½oz packages *ramyun* Korean instant noodles
2 eggs
vegetable oil, for deep-frying

TO SERVE
6 hamburger buns
¼ iceberg lettuce, shredded
⅓ cup mayonnaise, either ready-made or homemade
    (see page 83), divided
⅓ cup Korean Sweet Chile Sauce (see page 86), divided

1_ Put the chicken thighs in a large bowl and add the brine. Transfer to the refrigerator and let stand in the brine for 1 hour.

2_ After 1 hour, drain the chicken thighs and rinse them under cold running water to remove the excess salt left from the brine, then pat dry with paper towels.

3_ Break the instant noodles into small chunks and put in a food processor. Pulse until the noodles are fully broken down and are a similar size to bread crumbs, then tip the noodle "crumbs" onto a large plate. Crack the eggs into a small bowl and whisk together.

4_ Half-fill a large saucepan or deep-fryer with vegetable oil and preheat to 350°F, or until a cube of bread dropped in the oil browns in 30 seconds.

5_ Dip a chicken thigh first in the egg and then in the noodle "crumbs," ensuring it is completed coated. Shake off any excess noodle coating, then repeat with the remaining thighs.

6_ Lower the chicken thighs carefully into the hot oil and cook for 6 to 7 minutes. Lift the chicken out of the oil and let rest for 5 minutes, then carefully lower it back into the oil and fry for a further 3 to 4 minutes, until the noodle coating is golden brown and crunchy. Drain the chicken on paper towels to get rid of the excess oil.

7_ Slice the buns in half and arrange them, cut-side down, in a large dry skillet over high heat for 30 to 40 seconds, until warmed through and slightly charred at the edges.

8_ To assemble, arrange the shredded lettuce on the toasted bottom half of the buns. Spoon over some mayo, then top each bun half with a chicken thigh. Dollop over some chile sauce, sandwich together with the bun lid, and enjoy in big, messy mouthfuls.

Pomegranate-glazed Lamb Kebabs

Kebabs have become increasingly popular in Seoul. We'd noticed a few kebab outlets popping up in the expat district of Itaewon some years back and now, as street food, kebabs have started to make their way into mainstream areas, such as Myeong Dong, too. This isn't much of surprise since kebabs are essentially just grilled meats, so they work really well with all the typical Korean accompaniments. The pomegranate juice here gives this marinade a tart fruitiness, while the mango *kimchi* brings a really nice sweetness to the lamb. It's the kind of messy food that feels like it should be really bad for you. However, as fast food goes, it's actually a pretty healthy option.

MAKES 4

1lb 6oz boneless lamb leg, cut into 1¼-inch cubes
4 scallions, trimmed and cut into thirds
1 red bell pepper, cored, seeded, and cut into
   1¼-inch cubes
12 garlic cloves, minced
¼ cup regular soy sauce
½ cup pomegranate juice

¼ cup liquid honey
2 teaspoons apple vinegar
1 tablespoon vegetable oil

4 bamboo skewers, soaked in water for at least
   10 minutes

TO SERVE
4 pieces of pitta bread
¼ iceberg lettuce, shredded
4½oz Mango *Kimchi* (see page 38)
1 cup plain yogurt

1_ Mix all the ingredients except the vegetable oil together in a large bowl, cover with plastic wrap and let stand in the refrigerator to marinate for at least 30 minutes.

2_ When you are ready to cook, thread the bell pepper, lamb, and scallion pieces onto the skewers in an alternating pattern, leaving about 2 inches empty at either end (this will give you something to hold onto when you turn them over during cooking). Set the remaining marinade to one side.

3_ Brush a cast-iron ridged grill pan with the vegetable oil and place over medium-high heat.

4_ Carefully lay the kebabs on the grill and cook for 3 to 4 minutes on each of the four sides, brushing occasionally with the marinade, until the lamb is nicely browned and cooked to your liking. Remove from the heat and set aside for 2 minutes to rest.

5_ While the kebabs are resting, add the pitta breads to the pan to heat through for 30 seconds on each side.

6_ To serve, split the four pieces of pitta bread open and stuff each with a handful of lettuce. Slide the kebab pieces off the skewers and pile into the pitta bread along with the mango *kimchi* and yogurt.

Go Galbi BROILED MACKEREL

Translating as "mackerel ribs," this is a typical Busan dish, where the mackerel gets really crispy, so you can pick the fish up by the spines and eat the flesh as you would a meat rib. Though not for the faint-hearted, when the bones are really crisp like this you can even eat them whole.

SERVES
2

1 mackerel, weighing about 13oz
pinch of salt
2 to 3 tablespoons *Yangnyum Jang* (see page 21), to serve

1_ Cut along the belly of the mackerel with a sharp knife or scissors, remove the guts and wash the cavity clean. Remove the head and fins.

2_ Working from the inside of the mackerel belly, run a knife down either side of the spine until you reach the tail, then pull the fish open like the pages of a book, keeping the spine intact.

3_ Cover a large broiler pan with aluminum foil and preheat the broiler to high.

4_ Place the mackerel on the foil skin-side down and sprinkle with the salt. Broil for 5 minutes, then flip the mackerel over and broil flesh-side down for a further 5 minutes until the skin is browned and the fish is cooked through.

5_ Transfer to a large plate and serve drizzled with the *yangnyum jang*.

Korean Chile Crab

My family have been going to Jin Go Gae, a Korean restaurant in New Malden, in southwest London, for the past five or six years. It's not particularly conveniently located and it's pretty far from any station, but it's known to be one of the best and most authentic Korean restaurants around. In fact, my parents still travel up from Portsmouth to eat there almost every month, and the restaurant is always full. One of my favorite dishes there is a spicy marinated raw crab dish called *yangnyum gejang*. In Korea, this dish is nicknamed "the rice thief," because the sauce is so good that you keep going back for more rice to mop it up. Though I love it, raw crab isn't for everyone, so this is our version. It's addictive, messy, and delicious.

SERVES
2

1 large whole brown crab, or 2 small crabs, about 3lb 5oz in total
½ cup cooked short-grain rice (see page 26)
2 scallions, trimmed and thinly sliced, to garnish

SAUCE
2 tablespoons regular soy sauce
¼ cup *gochugaru* (Korean red chile powder)
1 tablespoon corn syrup
¼-inch piece of fresh ginger root, peeled and minced
1 tablespoon sesame oil
1 tablespoon mirin

4 garlic cloves, minced
1 tablespoon fish sauce
1 tablespoon apricot jam
1 tablespoon white rice vinegar
1 tablespoon roasted sesame seeds

1_ If you're cooking a live crab, put it in the freezer for 20 minutes to numb it prior to cooking.

2_ Fill a large pot with water and bring it to a vigorous boil. Fully submerge the crab into the water and cook for 12 minutes. Remove the crab from the water and set aside to cool.

3_ While the crab is cooling, make the sauce by mixing together all the ingredients in a bowl.

4_ Once the crab is cool, remove the legs and claws by gently twisting them off from where they meet the body. Set aside 3 tablespoons of the sauce and put the remaining sauce in a large bowl. Crack each of the legs and claws with a nutcracker or by hitting them swiftly with a large knife and then put these into the bowl with the sauce.

5_ Lay the crab on its back and carefully push a knife between the shell and central body part (or "purse") of the crab to prise it open. Set the purse aside. Drain off any water left behind in the shell, then remove and discard the circle of gray feathery gills (known as "dead man's fingers").

6_ Using a teaspoon, scoop out the remaining brown crabmeat from the inside of the shell and spoon it into a small bowl. Mash the crabmeat with a fork, add the rice and the remaining sauce, and mix together thoroughly. Set aside.

7_ Rinse the shell out under running water and dry thoroughly.

8_ Cut the crab purse into quarters with a large knife. Pick out the white crabmeat and transfer it to a small bowl.

9_ Lay the cleaned shell on a serving dish and fill it with the brown crabmeat and rice mixture. Spoon over the white crabmeat and garnish with the scallions.

10_ Pile the spicy claws and legs around the dressed crab and serve immediately. Be sure to eat this with plenty of napkins—it's messy!

Ojingeo Bokkeum STIR-FRIED SPICY SQUID

With its addictively spicy sauce and tender, soft squid, *ojingeo bokkeum* is one of Korea's most popular squid dishes. It can be found on the menus of snack houses, served as a simple lunch with a side of rice, or placed in the middle of the table to share as a *banchan*.

SERVES 2

1 whole squid, weighing about 6oz, cleaned and quill removed (ask them to do this for you at the fish counter)
1 tablespoon vegetable oil
1 onion, finely sliced
½ carrot, cut into thin diagonal strips

1 scallion, trimmed and coarsely chopped
1 long red chile, trimmed and coarsely chopped
1 teaspoon roasted sesame seeds, to garnish

SAUCE
1 tablespoon *gochujang* (Korean red chile paste)

2 tablespoons *gochugaru* (Korean red chile powder)
3 garlic cloves, minced
1 tablespoon mirin
1 tablespoon regular soy sauce
1 tablespoon superfine sugar
2 tablespoons water, plus extra if needed

1_ Slice the squid tube open to lay it flat, then run the tip of your knife along the squid lightly in a diagonal criss-cross pattern (this will help the squid curl up nicely while cooking). Cut the squid into 1-inch squares.

2_ For the sauce, mix all the ingredients together in a bowl.

3_ Heat the oil in a skillet over medium heat. Add the onion and carrot and fry for 3 to 4 minutes, stirring occasionally, until softened.

4_ Add the squid, scallion, chile, and sauce to the pan. Fry for 2 to 3 minutes, stirring, until the squid is tender and cooked through, adding another tablespoon or two of water if the sauce looks like it is getting too sticky and reduced. Scatter with the sesame seeds and serve.

Shrimp Po' Boy with Yuja Mayo

Gareth had always wanted to add a take on a po' boy to our menu because he's a big fan of this style of American sandwich, but it took us a while to decide on the filling. The breakthrough came when we were hosting a popup one summer at Old Bengal Bar in East London and were able to dedicate some time to testing lots of different ideas. Stuffed full of juicy shrimp, fresh crispy lettuce, and lots of bright, citrussy mayo, this is Gareth's idea of the perfect sandwich.

SERVES 6

24 large raw whole shrimp (about 1½lb)
vegetable oil, for deep-frying
4 hoagie or firm submarine buns
½ iceberg lettuce, shredded
2 tomatoes, thinly sliced

YUJA MAYO
2 egg yolks
¼ teaspoon English mustard

1 tablespoon *yuja* (yuzu) juice
2 teaspoons lemon juice
pinch of salt
½ tablespoon apple vinegar
½ cup vegetable oil

COATING
½ cup all-purpose flour sifted with
    ½ teaspoon baking powder

½ cup potato starch
⅓ cup cornmeal
pinch of salt
1 teaspoon baking powder
¼ teaspoon garlic granules
2 tablespoons *gochugaru* (Korean red chile powder)

1_ For the *yuja* mayo, put the egg yolks, mustard, *yuja* juice, lemon juice, salt, and apple vinegar in a food processor and blend together. With the motor running, pour in the vegetable oil in a thin, steady stream until you have a thick, creamy mayonnaise. Set aside.

2_ Peel the shrimp and remove the heads. Using a small, sharp knife, make a shallow cut along the back of each shrimp, then lift out the dark vein with the knife tip. Rinse under cold running water and drain.

3_ Half-fill a large pot or deep-fryer with vegetable oil and preheat to 350°F, or until a cube of bread dropped into the oil browns in 30 seconds.

4_ Mix all the coating ingredients together in a large bowl. Add the shrimp and toss together to ensure they are thoroughly coated, then lower them gently into the hot oil and fry for 1½ minutes. Remove the shrimp from the oil, season with salt, and let drain on paper towels.

5_ Slice the buns open and slather with the mayo, then pile in the lettuce, tomato, and shrimp to serve.

California Rolls

While now I'm a complete convert, I'd never been that big a fan of California rolls—and definitely never really considered them particularly Korean—until I started working at Korea Foods. The girls in the office there would almost always eat lunch together and, on special occasions, we'd always have California rolls. Mrs. Kim (the mother hen of the group), would make sure to organize it the day before and everyone would bring in one of the roll elements, then on roll day itself all the different ingredients would be heaped in piles in the middle of the table, and everyone would dive in and make their own. I loved how everyone could assemble the rolls to their own taste and, most importantly, how this great sharing dish really brought everyone together.

SERVES 8

4 eggs
pinch of salt
½ tablespoon vegetable oil
9oz seafood sticks

4 teaspoons wasabi (or English mustard)
½ cup mayonnaise, either ready-made or homemade
  (see page 83)
2¼lb (about 6 cups) cooked short-grain rice (see page 26)

2 red bell peppers, cored, seeded, and finely sliced
4 ripe avocados, seeded and sliced lengthwise
24 dried *gim* (nori) seaweed sheets, cut into quarters
1 cup regular soy sauce, to serve

1_ Beat together the eggs with the salt in a bowl.

2_ Heat the vegetable oil in a heavy skillet over medium heat and pour in half the egg mixture. Tip the pan so that the eggs spread out evenly to create a large, thin omelet, then fry for 30 seconds on each side. Remove the omelet from the pan and set aside to cool, then repeat with the remaining beaten egg to create a second omelet. Once cool, slice the omelets into ½-inch thick strips.

3_ Shred the seafood sticks into fine strands, put in a bowl with the wasabi and mayonnaise, and mix everything together well.

4_ Add the rice to a large bowl. Arrange the omelet slices, seafood-stick mixture, and all the other ingredients on a large platter. Place it in the middle of the table alongside the rice so everyone can assemble their own rolls. To make one, lay a seaweed quarter in the palm of your hand and spread a tablespoon or so of the rice in the middle, then arrange any combination of the assembled ingredients on top. Roll up and dip in the soy sauce to eat.

TIP: I've only listed my favorite fillings here, though you can add whatever you prefer. Cucumbers, stir-fried *eomuk* (Korean fishcakes), canned tuna, and pickled mooli were all popular fillings on California roll day. If you're not a fan of avocado (I'm not), I'd really encourage you to try it here anyway because it gives the rolls a really great creamy texture and with all the other flavors, you won't really taste it in any case.

Soups & Stews

YOU
SCRATCH
WHERE
IT ITCHES

Soups and stews are the comfort food of Korea. Ask any Korean person what their favorite Korean food is and most of them will reply either doenjang jjigae or kimchi jjigae. These stews are often cooked at home rather than eaten in restaurants, and so many people have memories associated with eating these growing up.

Even though Korea might be best known for its barbecue, it's the soups and stews that provide the backbone of a Korean meal. Traditionally meat was always expensive in Korea, so big barbecues were reserved for special occasions and for eating out. Instead, a Korean home-cooked meal would normally consist of individual bowls of rice, a selection of *banchan*, and, almost always, some sort of soup or stew.

Salt is rarely used as a seasoning, so soups and stews are usually flavored with the Korean *jang* ingredients of *ganjang* (soy sauce), *gochujang* (Korean red chile paste), and *doenjang* (Korean soybean paste) instead. It's also important to use a good stock, such as the anchovy stock *Myeulchi Gookmul* (see page 22) as the base, because this gives the soups and stews plenty of depth.

There are so many different soups and stews available in Korea that we've only been able to include our absolute favorites in this book. They can be split into the following types:

Guk

Guk, pronounced "gook" are usually simple soups that are often only simmered for a short period of time. These soups are typically very light and can be served as palate cleansers, and include examples such as *Jo-Gae Guk* (see page 154), which is usually served alongside spicy dishes to cool the mouth down.

Tang

Tangs are thicker, slightly heavier soups. They are normally more substantial than *guks* because they'll often contain chunks of meat or fish and include examples such as *Mae-Un-Tang* (see page 148) and *Dak Bokkeum Tang* (see page 144).

Jjigae

Korean stews, *jjigae* are pure comfort food for a lot of Koreans because they encompass the family favorites of *Kimchi Jjigae* (see page 138) and *Doenjang Jjigae* (see page 141). *Jjigae* are often served in hot stone bowls to preserve their heat, so that the the stew arrives at the table still bubbling.

Jorim

Jorim refer to braised dishes such as *Godeungeo Jorim* (see page 152) where the meat or fish is the star of the show. These are usually served in a big dish in the middle of the table for everyone to share.

Jjim

Jjim refers to steaming or boiling in a flavored sauce or soup, often cooked in a pressure cooker in a Korea. The liquid in *jjims* such as *Mae-Un Jjim Dak* (see page 144) is usually then simmered down to reduce it to a thicker sauce to coat all the ingredients.

Kimchi Jjigae KIMCHI STEW

I'm always torn between whether this or *Doenjang Jjigae* (see page 141) is my favorite Korean dish. Both are real home-cooking comfort foods and are so easy to put together. In fact, I think this was the first Korean dish that my mom ever taught me to make. The recipe is really simple, but there are a few key elements to a great *kimchi jjigae*. Firstly, your *kimchi* must be very mature and fermented, almost vinegary and super-tangy, because a young kimchi won't flavor the broth enough, and you'll be left with a very watery dish. Secondly, it's essential that you fry the *kimchi* for at least 10 minutes to bring out all of its flavors and make this stew as rich and spicy as it can be. Thirdly, don't chop the *kimchi* too finely, because you want to make sure it will still have a nice crunch.

SERVES 4

1 tablespoon vegetable oil
1lb 10oz extra-mature *Baechu Kimchi* (see page 32),
    coarsely chopped
7oz pork belly, finely sliced

4 cups water
9oz firm tofu, cut into 2-inch squares
1 scallion, trimmed and sliced at an angle, to garnish

1_ Heat the oil in a large heavy saucepan or stockpot over medium heat.

2_ Take the *kimchi* out of its fermenting "juice," add to the pan, and fry for 10 minutes, stirring occasionally. Add the pork belly and 2 to 3 tablespoons of the *kimchi* juice and fry for another 5 minutes until the pork is browned and the liquid has evaporated.

3_ Pour the measurement water into the pan, bring to a simmer, and let cook, uncovered, for 30 minutes until reduced down. Lay the tofu squares evenly over the top of the stew, cover with a lid, and simmer for 3 to 4 minutes, until the tofu is heated through. Ladle into bowls and serve scattered with the scallion to garnish.

TIPS: The *kimchi* I use here is usually one that I've had in the refrigerator for so long that it's almost fizzy with sour, fermented flavors, but if you're using ready-made *kimchi* or your *kimchi* has only matured for a few weeks, mix half a chicken stock cube in with the *kimchi* as you fry it for extra flavor.

On days when I don't have pork belly in the house, I just drain a can of tuna and use this instead (add this just before the tofu or it'll break up too much if you stew it for too long). Tuna is such a popular substitute for meat in this recipe that, in Korea, you can even get "tuna for *kimchi jjigae*," which sometimes even comes in meat-shaped cubes!

Budae Jjigae ARMY BASE STEW

During the Korean War, food was scarce and meat in particular was considered a real luxury. When American soldiers brought Spam over to Korea in their ration packs, Koreans started cooking with it —along with other ingredients such as wieners and processed cheese—and created this hot, spicy stew. While the combination of instant noodles, Spam, wieners, and processed cheese might sound like they belong in a student's cupboard, they actually make a really hearty, warming meal. Last summer, I was lucky enough to be invited onto a BBC show to cook *Buddae Jjigae* for our Marines, to show them that the Spam in their ration packs actually had the potential to taste good! Most of them were surprisingly won over— it's a lot tastier than it sounds.

SERVES
4

1 tablespoon vegetable oil
3½oz Spam, sliced into thin squares
2 wieners, finely sliced
4 cups *Myeulchi Gookmul* (see page 22)
2 scallions, trimmed and finely sliced
3½oz ground pork
3½oz *Baechu Kimchi* (see page 32), coarsely chopped
3½oz ricecake disks for soup (optional)

4½oz package *ramyun* Korean instant noodles
2 to 3 slices processed cheese

SAUCE
2 tablespoons *gochugaru* (Korean red chile powder)
1 tablespoon *gochujang* (Korean red chile paste)
1 tablespoon light soy sauce
4 garlic cloves, minced

1 teaspoon superfine sugar
pinch of salt
pinch of pepper

1_ For the sauce, mix together all the ingredients in a bowl. Set aside.

2_ Heat the vegetable oil in a large saucepan or stockpot over medium heat. Add the sliced Spam and wieners and fry for 2 to 3 minutes until the edges begin to brown and crisp up. Then pour in the stock and bring to a boil.

3_ Add the sauce, scallions, ground pork, *kimchi,* and ricecakes, if using, to the pan. Reduce the heat to a simmer and cook for 10 minutes, stirring occasionally until the ground pork is cooked through.

4_ Gently lower the noodles onto the top of the simmering stew, being careful not to submerge them in the liquid (this will stop them from overcooking). Lay the cheese slices over the noodles and let simmer for another 2 minutes, then transfer the still-bubbling pan to a heatproof stand in the middle of the table or ladle into bowls and serve immediately.

TIP: Korean ricecake disks can be found in either the frozen or chilled section of Asian supermarkets. They don't have a lot of flavor, but have a great chewy texture and are really filling, so can help to make soups stretch a lot further.

Doenjang Jjigae KOREAN SOYBEAN STEW

For most Koreans, this is the ultimate comfort food. It's the dish that they crave when they think of home—and almost every Korean will say that their mom makes the best version they've ever tasted. My mom makes a really good *doenjang jjigae*, but it's actually my aunt who makes the best (sorry Umma!). She eats it for breakfast, lunch, and dinner, so she's got it down to a fine art. Koreans rarely write recipes down, so it's often a case of throwing everything in a pot, tasting it, and then adjusting it until it's perfect. This is the closest I can get to my aunt's version.

SERVES 4

1 quart *Myeulchi Gookmul* (see page 22)
7oz pork belly, finely sliced
½ onion, thinly sliced
½ bird's-eye chile, trimmed and thinly sliced
2 garlic cloves, sliced

½ tablespoon *gochujang* (Korean red chile paste)
1 tablespoon *gochugaru* (Korean red chile powder)
3 tablespoons *doenjang* (Korean soybean paste)
1 tablespoon *saeujeot* (salted fermented shrimp), optional

½ zucchini, halved lengthwise and cut into ½-inch slices
7oz firm tofu, cut into 2-inch squares

1_ Bring the stock to a boil in a large saucepan or stockpot. Add the pork, onion, chile, garlic, *gochujang, gochugaru, doenjang,* and *saeujeot,* if using, and stir together well. Reduce the heat to a simmer and cook for 5 minutes, then add the zucchini slices and cook for a further 10 to 12 minutes, until the zucchini has softened.

2_ Arrange the tofu squares evenly on the top of the stew, cover with a lid, and simmer for 3 to 4 minutes, until the tofu is heated through. Serve bubbling and steaming hot.

TIP: Feel free to adjust this recipe to your own taste. Mushrooms, clams, and potatoes are all common additions, although you can really add any vegetable, meat, or seafood you like. Who knows? Your version might turn out as good as my aunt's . . . maybe!

Soondubu Jjigae SPICY SILKEN TOFU STEW

This is my go-to order whenever I eat at a Korean restaurant. Spicy, punchy, and with a lovely creamy texture from the silken tofu that could change the minds of even the toughest of tofu cynics, it's pretty irresistible. The clams are the magic ingredient here, giving the stew an unbeatable depth of flavor.

SERVES 2 AS A MAIN

5½oz clams
1 tablespoon salt
1 tablespoon vegetable oil
3½oz beef for stew
½ onion, thinly sliced
½ zucchini, thinly sliced

4 to 5 fresh shiitake mushrooms, trimmed and finely sliced
2 bird's-eye chiles, finely sliced
4 cups *Myeulchi Gookmul* (see page 22)
9oz extra-soft silken tofu
2 eggs
1 scallion, trimmed and finely sliced, to garnish

SEASONING PASTE
1 teaspoon sesame oil
3 tablespoons *gochugaru* (Korean red chile powder)
6 garlic cloves, minced
1 tablespoon regular soy sauce

1_ Sort through the clam shells, discarding any that are broken or don't close when tapped gently. Put the remaining clams in a large bowl with the salt and cover with cold water. Cover with aluminum foil, transfer to the refrigerator, and let soak for 2 hours, then drain and rinse the clams thoroughly under cold running water.

2_ For the seasoning paste, mix together the sesame oil, *gochugaru*, garlic, and soy sauce in a bowl.

3_ Heat the vegetable oil in a large saucepan or stockpot over medium heat. Add the seasoning paste and fry for 2 minutes, making sure to keep stirring because it sticks easily, until fragrant. Add the beef and fry for another 2 to 3 minutes, stirring, until browned. Stir in the onion, zucchini, mushrooms, and chiles ensuring everything is evenly coated in the paste, then pour in the stock.

4_ Bring the soup to a boil, reduce the heat to a simmer, and cook gently for 5 minutes, until the vegetables have softened. Stir in the tofu and clams and simmer for 3 to 4 minutes, until the clams have opened (discard any that are still shut). Return to a boil, add the eggs, and stir through briefly, then remove from the heat. Ladle into bowls, scatter with the scallions, and serve bubbling hot.

Sogogi Gori Jjim BRAISED OXTAIL STEW

We came up with this dish one night when we were planning a Korean feast for some friends. We'd thought of cooking *galbi jjim* (a Korean short rib stew), but when we went to pick up our ingredients, we couldn't resist the big chunks of oxtail at the butcher's counter. Oxtail doesn't have a lot of meat to it, but its center is filled with bone marrow, which makes this sauce deliciously rich and glossy. Once cooked, the meat will be tender and juicy and will fall off the bone at the lightest touch. On a cold winter's night, you'd be hard pressed to find a better meal.

SERVES
6

2lb 10oz oxtail, cut into 2-inch chunks
2½ tablespoons all-purpose flour
pinch of salt
pinch of finely ground white pepper
2 tablespoons vegetable oil
1 onion, finely chopped
2 carrots, finely chopped
½-inch piece of fresh ginger root, peeled and minced
4 garlic cloves, minced

2 kiwifruit, peeled and finely chopped
1 tablespoon sesame oil
2 tablespoons superfine sugar
2 tablespoons Shaoxing rice wine
1 tablespoon *gochugaru* (Korean red chile powder)
3 dried chiles, halved
1 cup regular soy sauce
3⅓ cups water
3 tablespoons rice wine vinegar

1 scallion, trimmed and finely chopped

TO SERVE
cooked short-grain rice (see page 26)
Maneul Jangajji (see page 87)

1_ Preheat the oven to 325°F.

2_ Place the oxtail pieces in a large bowl. Add the flour, salt, and pepper and mix together with your hands, ensuring each oxtail piece is thoroughly coated.

3_ Heat the vegetable oil in a Dutch oven over high heat. Add the oxtail pieces and cook for 5 to 6 minutes, turning them over every couple of minutes, until nicely browned on all sides (you may need to do this in batches to avoid overcrowding them). Remove the oxtail pieces from the dish and set aside.

4_ Add the onions and carrots to the Dutch oven, lower the temperature to medium, and cook, stirring, for 3 to 4 minutes, until the onions turn translucent and the carrots begin to soften. Return the oxtail pieces to the Dutch oven along with all the remaining ngredients except for the rice wine vinegar and chopped scallion. Stir together well.

5_ Cover the Dutch oven with the lid and transfer to the oven. Cook for 4 hours, skimming off any excess fat that floats to the surface every 30 minutes or so, until the meat is tender and slips easily off the bone when pressed gently with a fork. If the meat is still quite firm at this point, return it to the oven for another 30 minutes until tender.

6_ Once the oxtail is ready, remove the meat and vegetables from the cooking liquid with a slotted spoon and set to one side. Put the Dutch oven back on the hob over high heat and simmer for about 10 minutes until the liquid has reduced by one-third and is thick and glossy. Return the oxtail and vegetables to the pan along with the rice wine vinegar and the scallions and stir together well. Serve with rice and *maneul jangajji* (see page 87).

Mae-Un Jjim Dak SOY-BRAISED CHICKEN

This braised chicken dish is particularly famous in the Korean city of Andong, where there is even a street with a row of restaurants dedicated to serving it. The version they serve there has a distinctly spicy kick, but if you prefer something a little milder and with a sweeter flavor, simply take out the chiles.

3½oz *dangmyeon* sweet potato noodles
(see page 162)
6 whole garlic cloves
3 scallions, trimmed and cut into thirds
2¼lb bone-in, skin-on chicken thighs or drumsticks
1½ quarts water, plus extra if needed

5 dried chiles, coarsely chopped
5 long red chiles, trimmed and sliced
2 carrots, cut into bite-sized chunks
2 floury potatoes, peeled and cut into bite-sized chunks

SAUCE
⅔ cup regular soy sauce
2 tablespoons light soy sauce
3 tablespoons superfine sugar
pinch of pepper
1½ teaspoons sesame oil

1_ Put the sweet potato noodles in a bowl, cover with boiling water, and let soak for 15 minutes until soft. Drain and rinse in cold water. Set aside.

2_ For the sauce, combine all the ingredients together in a small bowl.

3_ Put the garlic, scallions, chiles, and chicken pieces in a large, heavy saucepan or stockpot. Pour in the measurement water (the chicken should be just covered; if not add a little more water) and bring to a boil. Cook for 15 minutes, keeping the water at a vigorous boil, then ladle out and discard approximately 1 cup of the liquid from the pot. Stir in the sauce, reduce the heat to a simmer, and cook for 10 minutes, then add the carrots and potatoes and cook for another 10 minutes, until the vegetables are tender and cooked through.

4_ Stir the sweet potato noodles through the stew, then ladle it into a large serving dish. Place it in the middle of the table so that everyone can help themselves.

Dak Bokkeum Tang SPICY BRAISED CHICKEN

I first introduced *dak bokkeum tang* (sometimes known as *dak dori tang*) to Gareth as a Korean chicken curry. I guess it is sort of the Korean equivalent; it has plenty of flavor, lots of spice, and a lovely rich sauce. The chicken here should be tender, and the potatoes just a minute or so from falling apart. The potatoes are my favorite part of this dish because they soak up all the delicious flavors from the sauce so well that you'll be fishing them out before anyone else can get at them.

2¼lb bone-in, skin-on chicken thighs and legs
2 onions, finely sliced
2 potatoes, cut into 2-inch chunks
3¼ cups water

1 carrot, coarsely chopped
1 bell pepper, cored, seeded, and coarsely chopped

SAUCE
3 tablespoons *gochujang* (Korean red chile paste)

4 garlic cloves, minced
3 tablespoons *gochugaru* (Korean red chile powder)
2 tablespoons regular soy sauce
3 tablespoons superfine sugar

1_ Mix together all the sauce ingredients in a small bowl, then add to a large heavy saucepan or stockpot with the chicken, onion, and potatoes. Add the measurement water, bring to a simmer, and let cook uncovered, stirring occasionally, for 30 minutes.

2_ Stir in the carrot and pepper and simmer gently for another 30 minutes, until the potatoes are on the point of collapsing and the chicken is tender and almost falling off of the bone. Serve with rice.

MAE-UN JJIM DAK

Haemul Bol Jjim SPICY SEAFOOD STEW

My cousin Ji Hyun stayed with us in the UK for a few months one summer so that he could study English and, while he loved it here, the thing he really craved from home was this spicy cod stew. I don't think I'd even tried it back then, but I remember him speaking longingly about it. Having had it since, I can confirm that there really is nothing like it. The seafood gives the delicious spicy sauce loads of flavor, the cod just falls apart into flakes, and the beansprouts are soft and slippery. If you're a seafood lover, you'll love this.

SERVES 4 to 6

10½oz mussels
14oz beansprouts
1 cup *Myeulchi Gookmul* (see page 22)
7oz large raw whole shrimp
1lb cod fillet, boned and cut into 2-inch squares
1¾oz chives

cooked short-grain rice (see page 26), to serve

SAUCE
3 tablespoons *gochujang* (Korean red chile paste)
4 tablespoons *gochugaru* (Korean red chile powder)
2 tablespoons mirin

8 garlic cloves, finely sliced
1 tablespoon regular soy sauce
1 scallion, trimmed and finely chopped
1 tablespoon sweet rice flour or cornstarch

1_ Sort through the mussels, tapping any that are open lightly on a surface to see if they close up. Discard the ones that remain open, or any that are damaged. Pull off the beards and scrape any barnacles off using the back of a knife, then rinse.

2_ Bring a saucepan of water to a boil, drop in the beansprouts, and cook for 3 to 4 minutes until just tender. Drain and rinse under cold running water to cool. Set aside.

3_ Pour the stock into a large heavy saucepan and bring to a boil. Reduce the heat to a simmer, add the mussels and shrimp, and simmer for 3 minutes. Add the cod, cover the pan with a lid, and simmer for another 3 to 4 minutes until everything is cooked through and the mussels have opened (discard any that remain closed). Remove the pan from the heat and drain off most of the stock, leaving ⅔ cup behind in the pan.

4_ Mix the sauce ingredients together in a bowl. Set aside.

5_ Return the pan to medium-high heat, add the beansprouts, chives, and sauce and gently stir together, being careful not to break up the cod. Simmer for 3 to 4 minutes, until the chives have wilted and everything is heated through.

6_ Ladle the stew into a large sharing dish and serve in the middle of the table with lots of rice to mop up the spicy sauce.

Mae-Un-Tang FISH MARKET FISH STEW

This dish tastes like Korea to me, its deep-sea flavors conjuring up memories of time spent there in restaurants by the beach. If you order sushi (or *hwe* in Korean) in Korea, this dish is usually served at the end of the meal. The *ajummas* take all the remaining sushi from your table and boil it up along with the chile paste and any heads and bones from the fish. It's a fantastic way of making sure that nothing is wasted, though it does mean that you're often left with a soup that is full of bones and not a lot of fish! In this version there's plenty of fish to go around.

SERVES
6 to 8

2½ quarts *Myeulchi Gookmul* (see page 22)
1lb 5oz mooli, halved lengthwise and cut into ¼-in slices
1 to 2 whole red snapper(s), about 1lb 10oz in total, scaled, cleaned, and cut into 2-inch thick steaks (ask them to do this for you at the fish counter)
3 scallions, trimmed and coarsely chopped

1 long red chile, trimmed and coarsely chopped
1 zucchini, coarsely chopped

PASTE
½ tablespoon *gochujang* (Korean red chile paste)
½ tablespoon *doenjang* (Korean soybean paste)
3 tablespoons *gochugaru* (Korean red chile powder)

6 garlic cloves, minced
3 tablespoons light soy sauce
1½ tablespoons fish sauce
pinch of pepper

1_ For the paste, mix together all the ingredients in a bowl. Set aside.

2_ Pour the stock into a large heavy saucepan or stockpot and bring to a boil. Add the mooli, reduce to a simmer, and cook over very low heat for 7 to 8 minutes until the mooli begins to soften.

3_ Stir the paste through the broth, add the fish, scallions, chile, and zucchini and simmer for another 6 to 7 minutes, until the zucchini has softened and the fish is cooked through. Transfer the still-bubbling broth in the hot pan to a heatproof stand in the middle of the table for everyone to help themselves.

Sam Gye Tang CHICKEN AND GINSENG SOUP

Sam gye tang will always be one of Gareth's most memorable meals from our first trip to Korea together. We went hiking up one of the many mountains in Seoul with my family one weekend and, after a couple of hours, we were feeling pretty tired and ready to rest. As if by magic, we came across a clearing with a stream running directly in front of us. Across the stream, there were two restaurants. An *ajumma* came out of each, beckoning us over for lunch, so we crossed the bridge and settled on the least pushy of the two for an amazing meal of *dotori muk* (acorn jelly), *pajeon* (scallion pancake), and *sam gye tang*. I'm not sure if perhaps we were really hungry from our trek, or whether it was the fresh mountain air or the fact that the food was simply delicious, but *sam gye tang* quickly became one of Gareth's favorite dishes.

Traditionally, this soup is a summer dish that's eaten on the hottest days of the year (*Sambok*). The idea is that the ginseng causes the temperature of the body to rise, making you sweat and therefore cooling you down. For me, it is warming and comforting, making it perfect for a chilly winter's night.

SERVES
4

½ cup short-grain rice
1 whole chicken, about 3lb 5oz
10 whole garlic cloves, divided
3oz ginseng root, whole
½-inch piece of fresh ginger root, peeled and sliced

6 *jujube* (dried red dates)
3¼ quarts water, plus extra if needed

TO GARNISH
2 scallions, trimmed and finely sliced

TO SERVE
salt
finely ground white pepper

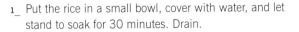

1_ Put the rice in a small bowl, cover with water, and let stand to soak for 30 minutes. Drain.

2_ If the chicken is trussed, remove any string and open out the legs. Stuff the cavity with the rice and half of the garlic cloves, then close up the cavity, folding any loose skin over the opening. Seal with a couple of toothpicks, skewering the skin shut.

3_ Place the chicken in a large, heavy saucepan or stockpot and add the gingseng, ginger, *jujube*, and the remaining garlic cloves. Pour in the measurement water until the chicken is just covered (adding more if necessary), cover with a lid, and bring to a boil. Boil vigorously for 30 minutes, then reduce the heat to simmer and cook for another 40 minutes until the chicken is cooked through.

4_ Garnish with the scallions and serve in the middle of the table with salt and freshly ground white pepper so that everyone can help themselves and season the chicken to their own taste.

TIP: This is often made from small squab chickens in individual portions, but we like to eat it as a sharing dish (like the one we had in the mountains). Give each person an empty bowl along with little dishes of salt and pepper, so they can take their favorite parts of the chicken, scoop out all the sticky rice from the inside, and season to their taste.

Godeungeo Jorim MACKEREL STEW

This was another one of those dinners that we would have a lot when I was growing up. Mom would whip it together really quickly without having to go to the grocery store. She always used canned mackerel, which we usually had in the cupboard at home. I like this dish with either fresh or canned mackerel, but the broth from the fresh mackerel always tastes a little livelier and the mackerel itself goes silky soft. The mooli is my favorite part of this stew, though, since it takes on all the flavors of the sauce. I love to mash it up with my rice, a little mackerel, and a few tablespoons of the liquid. I admit it may be a little uncouth, but it must be something I've picked up since my eldest uncle loves to do the same thing.

SERVES
6

2 mackerel, approximately 1lb 2oz in total
9oz mooli, halved lengthwise and
    cut into ½-inch thick slices
½ onion, finely sliced
2 long red chiles, coarsely chopped

SAUCE
3 tablespoons *gochugaru* (Korean red chile powder)
5 tablespoons regular soy sauce
2 garlic cloves, finely sliced
1 cup water

1_ Cut along the belly of the mackerel with a sharp knife or scissors, remove the guts, and wash the cavities clean. Remove the heads and fins and cut the mackerel into 1¼-inch chunks, leaving the bones in.

2_ For the sauce, mix together the ingredients in a bowl. Set aside.

3_ Arrange the mooli slices on the bottom of a heavy saucepan. Add the onion, chile, and mackerel pieces and pour in the sauce. Bring to a simmer, then cover and cook for 30 minutes until the mooli is soft and the mackerel is cooked through.

Miyuk Guk BIRTHDAY SEAWEED SOUP

Although it can be enjoyed anytime, *miyuk guk* is traditionally eaten as a celebratory birthday dish in Korea. In fact, because it's full of restorative nutrients, *miyuk guk* is one of the first dishes that new mothers eat after having a baby. On the other hand, if you're taking any exams this is one to be avoided because Koreans say that the seaweed is so slippery that you could fail as you might "slip up" (we're not pulling your leg). My mom loves this dish and its simplicity, whereas I like to add a tablespoon of *gochugaru* at the end for a bit of heat. This is slightly unusual—my cousin and I are the only people I know who eat it this way—but I swear it really lifts the soup. If you want to stick with tradition, leave it out.

SERVES
4

¾oz dried *miyuk* (wakame) seaweed
5½oz beefsteak for stew, diced
2 tablespoons light soy sauce
pinch of pepper

2 garlic cloves, minced
2 tablespoons sesame oil
4 cups water

TO SERVE
gochugaru (Korean red chile powder), to taste

1_ Put the seaweed in a small bowl, cover with cold water, and let stand for 10 to 15 minutes until soft and slippery. Drain and set aside.

2_ Meanwhile, put the beef in a large bowl with the soy sauce, pepper, and garlic. Mix all the ingredients together and set aside to marinate for 15 minutes.

3_ Once ready to cook, heat the sesame oil in a large saucepan or stockpot over medium heat. Add the beef to the pan and fry for 2 to 3 minutes, stirring, until browned on all sides. Add the seaweed and fry for another 2 minutes, stirring continuously to prevent the seaweed from sticking to the edges of the pan. Then pour in the measurement water and bring to a boil. Reduce the heat and simmer for 30 minutes. Serve with a bowl of chile powder to add to taste.

Jo-Gae Guk CLEAR CLAM SOUP

The best way to describe this soup is that it tastes just like the sea. It's light and fresh, so it's the perfect accompaniment to spicier, heavier dishes such as *Jeyuk Bokkeum* (see page 108) or *Ojingeo Bokkeum* (see page 129). This is probably one of the most stripped-back Korean dishes there is, with all the ingredients acting to just enhance the natural flavors of the clams very gently.

SERVES
4

1lb clams
2 tablespoons salt
3 dried *dashima* (kombu) kelp rectangles,
    about 2 x 1¼ inches in size

3 large dried anchovies
4 cups boiling water
1oz mooli, finely sliced
1 red chile, trimmed, seeded, and finely sliced
1 scallion, trimmed and finely sliced

1_ Sort through the clam shells, discarding any that are broken or don't close when tapped gently on a hard surface. Put the remaining clams in a large bowl with the salt and cover with cold water. Cover with aluminum foil, transfer to the refrigerator, and let soak for 2 hours, then drain and rinse the clams thoroughly under cold running water. Set aside.

2_ Place the dried kelp and anchovies in a large bowl with the measurement water and let soak for

10 minutes, then transfer to a large saucepan along with the soaking liquid. Add the mooli, chile, and scallion. Season with salt and bring to a boil.

3_ Once the mixture is boiling, remove the kelp and anchovies and discard. Add the clams and simmer for 2 to 3 minutes, skimming off any scum that floats to the surface with a spoon. The clams should now all be open; discard any that are still closed and serve immediately.

Dak Yukgaejang SPICY CHICKEN AND LEEK SOUP

Although this spicy soup is typically made with shredded beef, it never has been in our house. Instead it is always made with chicken or turkey, or more accurately, leftover roast chicken or roast turkey left over from Christmas dinner. Yet, while it may be my mom's equivalent of a Boxing Day turkey curry, it's so much more than just a leftovers dish. In fact, it's actually one of my dad's favorite Korean dishes. The soup is spicy and rich and I particularly love the leeks, which turn silken and slippery soft during cooking. Serve it simply with a side of white rice—and *kimchi*, of course.

SERVES
2

1 tablespoon vegetable oil
5½oz cooked chicken, shredded
¼ leek, trimmed, cleaned, and cut into 2-inch chunks
4 cups *Dak Yuksu* (see page 23)

PASTE
1 teaspoon sesame oil
3 tablespoons *gochugaru* (Korean red chile powder)
6 garlic cloves, minced
1 tablespoon regular soy sauce

TO SERVE
cooked short-grain rice (see page 26)
Baechu Kimchi (see page 32)

1_ For the paste, thoroughly mix together the ingredients in a small bowl.

2_ Heat the vegetable oil in a large saucepan or stockpot over medium heat. Add the seasoning paste and fry for 2 minutes, making sure to keep stirring—it sticks easily—until fragrant. Add the chicken to the pan, stirring to ensure it is thoroughly coated in the paste, and cook for another 2 minutes.

3_ Add the leek and pour in the *dak yuksu*. Bring to a simmer and cook for 15 minutes until the leeks are soft and silky. Serve with rice and *kimchi*.

Gamjatang HANGOVER STEW

Every country has a range of their own special hangover cures, and this is one of Korea's most popular. A hearty, meaty, spicy stew, it is (almost) guaranteed to clear your head after a heavy night. While *gamjatang* translates as "potato stew," this dish doesn't actually always have potatoes in it, the *gamja* (which ordinarily means "potato") referring instead to the knobbly pork spine that is traditionally used to make it. Here we've replaced this with pork ribs, which are much easier to find.

SERVES 6

7oz new potatoes, halved
2¼lb pork ribs
1 onion, coarsely chopped
2 scallions, trimmed and coarsely chopped
5 whole garlic cloves
1-inch piece of fresh ginger root, peeled and minced
2¾ quarts water
7oz *Baechu Kimchi* (see page 32), cut into thin strips and rinsed

1¾oz chives
4½oz enoki mushrooms, trimmed

SAUCE
2 tablespoons *gochugaru* (Korean red chile powder)
12 garlic cloves, finely sliced
1-inch piece of fresh ginger root, peeled and minced
1 tablespoon light soy sauce
1 tablespoon fish sauce
3 tablespoons mirin

1 tablespoon *gochujang* (Korean red chile paste)
3 tablespoons *doenjang* (Korean soybean paste)
3 tablespoons perilla seed powder (optional)

TO SERVE
cooked short-grain rice (see page 26)
Baechu Kimchi (see page 32)

1_ For the sauce, mix together the ingredients in a small bowl. Set aside.

2_ Bring a saucepan of water to a boil, add the potatoes, and cook for 15 minutes, or until just tender. Drain and rinse under cold running water to cool. Set aside.

3_ Place the ribs in a large saucepan or stockpot with the onion, scallion, garlic, and ginger. Cover with the measurement water, bring to a boil, and cook, uncovered, for 1 hour. Stir through the *kimchi* and sauce, reduce the heat to a simmer, and cook gently for 15 minutes, then add the potatoes, chives, and mushrooms and simmer for another 2 to 3 minutes until the potatoes have heated through and the chives have wilted.

4_ Ladle into bowls and serve with rice and *kimchi*.

TIP: Perilla seed powder is made from an herb of the mint family and gives this dish its unique flavor and a slightly numbing, tingly heat. It can be found in Korean supermarkets, but if you can't get hold of it, use a couple of teaspoons of finely ground black pepper instead.

07

Rice & Noodles

If you talk about a

TIGER

IT WILL COME

RICE

Rice is a key part of a Korean diet, so much so that the Korean word for rice, *bap* is the same as the word for food.

Unless noodles are served, short-grain, white (sushi) rice is eaten at every meal and most Koreans will feel like they haven't had a complete meal unless they've eaten a bowl. In fact, even when we go out for Korean BBQ and have had our fill of meat, my family still often orders a few bowls of rice to eat with a *jjigae* to finish the meal.

Korean rice can be eaten plain, mixed with vegetables and *gochujang* to create *bibimbap*, or fried to make *bokkeumbap*. In Korea, it's even used as a vehicle for different fillings like a sandwich in the form of *Kimbap*. It can also be turned into the following:

Juk

Rice is often simmered with plenty of water to create a kind of porridge known as *juk*. This is usually eaten when you're feeling unwell, or by the elderly, because it's easy to eat and digest.

Rice Flour and Ricecakes

Rice can be ground to make a flour (such as sweet rice flour), which can then be used to make Korean ricecakes called *tteok*. Rice flour is also an important ingredient in fermenting *kimchi* and making batters.

Nurungji

During boiling, rice can often scorch and stick to the bottom of the pan creating a thin layer of crispy rice known as *nurungji*. *Nurungji* can be eaten as a crunchy snack (sometimes dusted with a little sugar), or water can be poured into the pan and brought to a boil to create *sungnyung*, which is sometimes eaten after a meal to aid digestion.

Alcohol

Korea's biggest-selling spirit *soju* was traditionally made from rice (though it's now often made from a combination of grains and starches). *Soju* is a clear spirit, around 20 percent alcohol by volume (ABV) and has a slightly sweet, clean flavor that particularly complements spicy or salty foods. Another popular alcohol in Korea is called *makgeolli*, which is a rice beer. This creamy drink is made from uncooked rice and a fermentation starter called *nuruk*.

NOODLES

I eat rice almost every day, so I think I'd find it impossible to live without it. It's my comfort food and, particularly when I'm feeling unwell, all I want is a bowl of rice and kimchi. My mom, however, could probably give it up as long as she had noodles in her life. Noodles are my mom's favorite thing to eat, and though she has quite a small appetite the rest of the time, sit her in front of a bowl of noodles and she'll be able to eat them faster than anyone else. There are so many different types of noodles in Korea, so if my mom did give up rice, she'd have plenty of choice. Those we've mentioned in this book include:

Somyun

Somyun are thin vermicelli noodles made from flour. They're quite starchy, so need to be cooked separately and then rinsed and drained before being added to any soups. *Somyun* noodles can be eaten either hot, as in *Janchi Guksu*, a clear soup traditionally eaten at celebrations, or cold in chilled noodle salads like *Bibim Guksu* (see page 175).

Naengmyeon

Naengmyeon are springy buckwheat noodles that originate from the northern parts of Korea. These noodles are similar to Japanese soba noodles, but they contain sweet potato starch, which gives them a bouncier, chewier texture. The noodles are slippery (not starchy) and are always enjoyed cold, whether with a spicy sauce or added to a chilled broth like *Mul Naengmyeon* (see page 176).

Dangmyeon

Dangmyeon are also sometimes known as cellophane or glass noodles because they go glossy and transparent when cooked. These noodles are made from sweet potato starch and are usually sold dried in big packages, so they need to be rehydrated in plenty of water before cooking. *Dangmyeon* are the key ingredient in *Japchae* (see page 168) but they're also used in other recipes too, often cut into small pieces to add a little chewy texture, as in the filling for *Gogi Mandu* (see page 53).

Kalguksu

Kalguksu translates as "knife noodles," since these noodles are traditionally rolled out in large sheets and then cut by hand with a sharp knife. These noodles can also be bought dried, but the texture is very different, so it's best to make your own at home (see page 173). *Kalguksu* are chewy, starchy, and very filling.

Ramyun

Ramyun refers to Korean instant noodles. They're so popular in Korea, we absolutely had to include them here! *Ramyun* are usually wheat noodles that have been pre-fried and come in a large package, along with some dried vegetables and a seasoning sachet, which creates (an often spicy) noodle broth. The noodles are usually quite springy in texture. *Ramyun* are a quick, cheap, and convenient option for many Koreans.

A note on noodles: Long noodles are said to symbolize a long life so, for this reason, a lot of people (including my uncle) say that you shouldn't cut them, the idea being that you wouldn't want to cut your life short.

Kimchi Bokkeumbap *KIMCHI*-FRIED RICE

Of all the recipes in this book, this is probably the one that we eat the most often. It's the perfect midweek dinner because it's really quick and easy to cook. We usually have all the ingredients in our refrigerator and it's a great way to use up leftover rice, since fresh rice here will just make everything a little mushy. The egg on top is a must—I like mine just-cooked and really runny, so that the yolk mixes into the rice and becomes the sauce. Perfect.

SERVES
2

1 tablespoon vegetable oil, plus extra for frying
3½oz pork belly, finely chopped
5½oz *Baechu Kimchi* (see page 32)
1 tablespoon sesame oil
2 cups cooked short-grain rice (see page 26)

1 tablespoon sesame seeds
1 tablespoon *Gochugaru* (Korean chile powder)
2 scallions, trimmed and finely sliced
2 eggs

1_ In a heavy skillet, heat the vegetable oil over medium heat.

2_ Add the pork belly pieces to the pan and cook for 2 to 3 minutes, stirring, until the edges begin to crisp up and the pork is cooked through. Add the *kimchi* and stir-fry for another 2 to 3 minutes, then add the sesame oil, rice, sesame seeds, and chile powder and continue to cook, stirring, until the rice is completely heated through. Stir in the scallions (reserving a little for garnish) and spoon into bowls.

3_ While the rice is still hot, quickly fry the eggs to your liking in a separate pan. Place a fried egg on the top of each rice bowl and garnish with the reserved scallions.

Dolsot Bibimbap KOREAN MIXED RICE

Bibimbap literally translates as "mixed rice" (*bibim* = mixed, *bap* = rice), so you can actually throw any ingredients together with some rice and you'd have a form of *bibimbap*. My mom usually makes hers with leftover rice, *Miyuk Muchim* and *Kongnamul Muchim* (see pages 60 and 61) mixed together with some *gochujang* and sesame oil for a quick lunch.

This recipe is the fancier version—*dolsot* refers to the hot stone bowl that the rice is served in. It's served sizzling hot with a raw egg in the middle, which you mix in at the end so you have the texture combination of crispy and soft rice, crunchy vegetables, and soft, runny egg. If you don't have a stone bowl, then you can still get the crispiness by flattening the rice into an even layer in a skillet instead.

SERVES
2

---

2 to 3 dried shiitake mushrooms
vegetable oil
½ carrot, cut into matchsticks
½ zucchini, cut into matchsticks
3½oz *Sigeumchi Muchim* (see page 60)

3½oz *Kongnamul Muchim* (see page 60)
2¾ cups cooked short-grain rice (see page 26)
1 tablespoon sesame oil
1 egg
salt

SAUCE
2 tablespoons *gochujang* (Korean red chile paste)
1 tablespoon sesame seeds
2 tablespoons sesame oil
½ tablespoon superfine sugar
2 garlic cloves, minced

1_ Put the shiitake mushrooms in a bowl and cover with boiling water. Let soak for 10 minutes, then strain and slice into thin strips.

2_ Mix all the sauce ingredients together in a small bowl. Set aside.

3_ Heat a splash of oil in a heavy skillet over medium heat. Add the carrot, season with salt, and cook, stirring, for 2 to 3 minutes until the carrot has softened slightly. Set the carrot aside and repeat with the zucchini.

4_ To assemble the dish, heat a Korean *dolsot* stone bowl or a heavy skillet over high heat for 3 to 4 minutes until really hot. Brush the inside of the bowl or pan with the sesame oil, then add the rice, pressing it down onto the bottom and up the sides so as much of the surface as possible gets covered (this will ensure you get lots of crispy bits).

5_ Once the rice starts to sizzle, start arranging the vegetables in neat piles around the edges, leaving it over high heat and allowing it to cook for another 2 minutes to ensure the rice is nice and crisp. Crack the egg in the center of the *dolsot* or pan, and carefully remove it from the heat. Serve piping hot, but keep the sauce separate so that you can make your portion as spicy as you like.

TIP: If you want to make this meaty, add around 1¾oz of *Yukhoe* (see page 100) to each bowl along with the vegetables. The heat of the hot stone bowl will quickly sear the beef once it's stirred through, so it'll be nicely browned on the outside but still pink in the middle.

Japchae STIR-FRIED "ROYAL" NOODLES

Along with *bulgogi* and *kimchi*, this is probably one of Korea's most popular and well-known dishes. Historically, these stir-fried sweet potato noodles were enjoyed exclusively by royalty, but now they can be found on any Korean table, particularly when friends and family gather together in celebration. In fact, it's my mom's go-to party-platter dish because it's easy to whip up and can be enjoyed both hot and cold.

SERVES
4
AS AN APPETIZER

SERVES
2
AS A MAIN

4 dried shiitake mushrooms
3½oz beefsteak for frying, cut into ¼-inch slices
5½oz *dangmyeon* sweet potato noodles
3 tablespoons vegetable oil, divided
½ carrot, cut into matchsticks
1 red bell pepper, cored, seeded, and thinly sliced
2 scallions, trimmed and cut into 2-inch lengths
3½oz *Sigeumchi Muchim* (see page 60)

MARINADE
1 tablespoon regular soy sauce
2 garlic cloves, minced
2 teaspoons superfine sugar
pinch of pepper

SAUCE
1 tablespoon sesame oil
¼ cup regular soy sauce
2 teaspoons superfine sugar
2 tablespoons roasted sesame seeds,
     plus extra to garnish
1 garlic clove, minced
pinch of pepper

1_ Put the shiitake mushrooms in a bowl and cover with boiling water. Let soak for 10 minutes, then strain and slice into thin strips.

2_ Meanwhile, mix the marinade ingredients together in a bowl. Add the beef slices and mix well to ensure everything is evenly coated, then let marinate for 10 minutes.

3_ Combine the sauce ingredients in another bowl and set aside.

4_ Cook the noodles in boiling water following the package directions, then drain well and rinse under cold water.

5_ Heat 1 tablespoon of vegetable oil in a large skillet over medium heat. Add the marinated beef slices and fry for 1 to 2 minutes until browned, then remove from the pan and set aside.

6_ Add the carrot to the pan and fry for 2 minutes until softened, then add the bell pepper and scallions and fry for another 2 minutes. Remove the vegetables from the pan and set aside, keeping the pan over the heat.

7_ Pour the remaining 2 tablespoons of vegetable oil into the pan, then add the noodles and cook, stirring, for 2 minutes until the noodles are heated through. Add the sauce and all the other ingredients and stir-fry for another 2 minutes, making sure everything is mixed together and is evenly coated with the sauce.

8_ Divide between bowls, garnish with a few extra sesame seeds, and serve immediately.

KNIFE-CUT NOODLES STEP-BY-STEP

1_ See page 173 for ingredients. Using a rolling pin, roll the dough out into a large rectangular shape, dusting with plenty of flour as you go, until it is about ⅛ inch thick. (Be warned! You'll need a large space.)

2_ Run a knife along the outside of the rectangle to straighten the edges and remove any excess dough (this will help you to get even noodles).

3_ Starting from one of the narrow ends of the rectangle, fold over 4 inches of the dough. Dust with flour.

4_ Fold and dust with flour again, then repeat until you have reached the other end and are left with a block of dough with layers of folds.

5_ Using a sharp knife, cut the dough block widthwise into ¼-inch strips.

6_ Unfold the noodles and dust them with flour. Cover with plastic wrap and set aside until needed. The dough can be made a day ahead but the noodles are best eaten on the day they are rolled and cut.

Kalguksu KNIFE-CUT NOODLES

There's a whole row of stands in Namdaemun market in Seoul called "*Kalguksu* Alley," where all the *ajummas* are hidden by clouds of steam, huddled over big pans of bubbling stock, each making *kalguksu* following their own special recipe. My favorite place to enjoy this noodle broth, though, is a standalone hut in the middle of the hustle and bustle of the main market. Here, the *ajummas* are amazingly skilled, deftly making noodles at amazing speed, thanks to their years of experience. There are faded menus on the walls displaying a selection of different dishes, but everyone comes here to eat the noodles. Each table has a little earthenware pot of very fermented *kimchi* that you help yourself to—the tangy chile heat cuts through the starchy, chewy noodles and is the perfect match.

SERVES
4

2¼ quarts *Dak Yuksu* (see page 23)
1 zucchini, cut into thin matchsticks
3½oz cooked chicken meat, shredded

NOODLES
5 cups all-purpose flour, plus extra for dusting
¼ cup sweet rice flour

2 teaspoons salt
1¼ cups water

TO GARNISH
1 dried *gim* (nori) seaweed sheet, finely sliced
2 tablespoons roasted sesame seeds
1 scallion, trimmed and finely sliced

TO SERVE
Yangnyum Jang (see page 21)
matured *Baechu Kimchi* (see page 32)

1_ To make the noodles, in a large bowl combine the flour, rice flour, and salt. Add the water a little at a time and stir together with a wooden spoon until the mixture begins to stick together. Using your hands, shape the mixture into a rough ball, then set it onto a clean, floured surface. Knead it for 10 minutes until the dough is smooth and elastic.

2_ Wrap the dough ball in clingfilm and refrigerate for 20 minutes, then return the dough to the floured work surface and knead for another 10 minutes, adding a little extra flour as you go to stop the dough from sticking. Roll out and cut the noodles following the step-by-step instructions on the previous page.

3_ Bring the stock to a vigorous boil in a large saucepan. Add the zucchini and cooked chicken and cook for 2 minutes until the zucchini has softened. Add the noodles to the pan and boil for 3 minutes, or until the noodles are cooked through, stirring using a fork or pasta tongs to stop the noodles from sticking together.

4_ Ladle the noodles into large bowls, scatter with the seaweed, sesame seeds, and scallion to garnish and serve with *yangnyum jang* and strong *baechu kimchi*, so that each person can adjust their portion to their own taste.

Dangmyeon Bokkeum SPICY STIR-FRIED VEGETABLE NOODLES

Strangely enough, this vegetarian- and vegan-friendly dish is actually based on *soondae bokkeum*, a real meat-eater's meal made with a blood sausage called *soondae*, the Korean version of black pudding. This adaptation focuses on the dish's best part, its spicy sauce, which clings here to the sweet potato noodles, making them deliciously sticky and irresistible to even the most hardcore carnivore.

SERVES 4

10 dried shiitake mushrooms
5½oz *dangmyeon* sweet potato noodles
⅓ cup vegetable oil, divided
1 eggplant, cut into ½-inch cubes
2 garlic cloves, minced
2 bird's-eye chiles, trimmed and chopped
pinch of salt
1 onion, thinly sliced
½ red cabbage, thinly sliced

1lb 2oz cremino mushrooms, sliced

SAUCE
2 tablespoons *gochugaru* (Korean red chile powder)
2 tablespoons *gochujang* (Korean red chile paste)
2 tablespoons regular soy sauce
2 tablespoons sesame oil
2 tablespoons liquid honey
6 garlic cloves, minced

1 tablespoon *soju* (Korean rice spirit) or mirin
2 tablespoons apple vinegar
2 tablespoons perilla seed powder or 2 teaspoons finely ground black pepper

TO GARNISH
2 scallions, trimmed and finely chopped
2 tablespoons roasted sesame seeds
1 dried *gim* (nori) seaweed sheet, sliced into thin matchsticks

1_ Put the shiitake mushrooms in a bowl and cover with boiling water. Let soak for 10 minutes, then strain, setting aside the soaking water, and slice into thin strips.

2_ Meanwhile, cook the noodles in boiling water following the package directions, then drain well and rinse under cold water. Set aside.

3_ To make the sauce, put all the ingredients together in a bowl and mix together well, stirring in a tablespoon of the mushroom soaking water to loosen the mixture a little.

4_ Heat half of the vegetable oil in a large skillet over medium heat. Add the eggplant and cook, stirring, for 3 minutes until softened, then add the garlic, chiles, and salt and cook for another 2 to 3 minutes. Transfer the eggplant to a plate and set aside.

5_ Put the pan back over medium heat. Add the remaining vegetable oil. Add the onion, lower the heat, and cook gently, stirring occasionally, for 10 minutes, until the onion is softened but not brown.

6_ Add the shiitake mushrooms to the pan along with the cabbage and cremino mushrooms. Increase the heat to medium and stir-fry for 5 to 6 minutes, then add the noodles and sauce, tossing or stirring everything together so that the noodles are completely coated and the ingredients are evenly distributed. Continue cooking for 2 to 3 minutes until the noodles are heated through, stirring to ensure they don't stick to the bottom of the pan.

7_ Garnish with scallion, sesame seeds, and seaweed strips to serve.

Bibim Guksu SUMMER NOODLE SALAD

These spicy noodles are a great way to use up any leftover salad ingredients or crunchy vegetables you may have lurking in your refrigerator, so don't feel bound by the carrots and iceberg lettuce we use here. My mom likes to add the (slightly unusual) combination of arugula and watercress to hers to give it a really peppery kick. Serving this with the Korean egg drop soup will help extinguish some of the heat.

SERVES
2

6oz *somyun* vermicelli noodles
1 green apple, cored and cut into thin strips
¼ iceberg lettuce, shredded
1 carrot, halved and cut into thin strips
1 scallion, trimmed and finely sliced, plus extra
   to garnish
3 tablespoons *gochujang* (Korean red chile paste)
1 tablespoon *gochugaru* (Korean red chile powder)

2 garlic cloves, minced
1½ tablespoons superfine sugar
3½ tablespoons apple vinegar
1 teaspoon roasted sesame seeds
1 teaspoon sesame oil
2 hard-boiled eggs, peeled and sliced, to garnish

GYERAN GUK (KOREAN EGG DROP SOUP)
2 cups *Myeulchi Gookmul* (see page 22)
1 tablespoon light soy sauce
2 scallions, trimmed and finely chopped
2 eggs, beaten

TO SERVE
English mustard
apple vinegar

1_ Cook the noodles in boiling water following the package dirctions, then drain well and rinse under cold water.

2_ Squeeze out any excess water from the noodles and put them into a large bowl with all the remaining ingredients except the hard-boiled eggs. Mix everything together well, then divide between bowls.

3_ For the *gyeran guk*, put the stock in a saucepan with the soy sauce and scallions and bring to a boil. Add the beaten egg to the boiling stock, using a chopstick or a spoon to ensure the ribbons are distributed evenly through the liquid. Allow the egg to cook for 20 to 30 seconds until lightly cooked, then pour into side bowls.

4_ Garnish the *bibim guksu* with the hard-boiled egg slices and a little extra scallion. Serve with the soup, along with mustard and vinegar to season to taste.

Mul Naengmyeon CHILLED NOODLE SOUP

Along with *Bibim Guksu* (see page 175) this is one of my favorite things to eat in the summer. Made from buckwheat, these noodles are springy and chewy—a completely different texture to the soft *somyun* vermicelli noodles typically used in Korean soups. I like to add loads of vinegar and mustard to the ice cold broth here, often so much that it makes me suck in my cheeks and gives me a severe case of "mustard nose."

SERVES 2

9oz *naengmyeon* buckwheat noodles
10 ice cubes, crushed
½ Asian pear, peeled, cored, and thinly sliced
5½oz beefsteak for frying, thinly sliced and
    cooked to your liking
2 hard-boiled eggs, peeled

BROTH
2 cups beef stock
3 whole garlic cloves

¾-inch piece of fresh ginger root, whole
1 scallion, trimmed and coarsely chopped
1 tablespoon light soy sauce
2 tablespoons apple vinegar

SAUCE
½ Asian pear, peeled, cored, and puréed
1 scallion, trimmed and finely sliced
1 tablespoon regular soy sauce
1 tablespoon *gochugaru* (Korean red chile powder)

1 teaspoon superfine sugar
1 teaspoon apple vinegar
2 garlic cloves, minced
½-inch piece of fresh ginger root, peeled and minced
½ teaspoon roasted sesame seeds

TO SERVE
English mustard
apple vinegar

1_ Add all of the broth ingredients to a large saucepan over high heat and bring to a boil. Reduce the heat and simmer over medium heat for 10 minutes, then strain the broth through a sieve. Pour the strained broth into a large bowl and let chill in the refrigerator for about 30 minutes until cooled.

2_ While the stock is chilling, mix the sauce ingredients together in a small bowl. Set aside.

3_ Cook the noodles in boiling water following the package directions, then drain well and rinse under cold running water.

4_ Divide the ice cubes, noodles, pear, and steak between two serving bowls, then pour half of the chilled stock over each.

5_ Halve the eggs and arrange on top of the noodles. Spoon over the sauce and serve with English mustard and apple vinegar on the side for adding to the broth as you like.

Ramyun INSTANT NOODLES

> *Ramyun* (or instant noodles) are so loved by Koreans that they consume more of them per head than anyone else in the world. In most corner stores in Korea you'll find a *ramyun* area where you can take your cup of instant noodles, fill it at the hot water station, and sit down on a plastic bench to eat your speedy meal. To Koreans, *ramyun* are more than a quick and easy fast food, though. People genuinely love the taste, and most have their own way of customizing them to turn them into a hearty and substantial meal. We've included our favorite ways of eating these noodles here, as well as asking some of our friends how they eat theirs. We also recommend using Korean instant noodles in a hot and spicy flavor. We normally eat the *Shin Ramyun* brand at home, so the recipes below are based on this.

JUDY JOO'S *RAMYUN*
Executive Chef of Jinjuu Restaurant

Throw away your noodle seasoning sachet and make your own broth by mixing 2 tablespoons *gochujang* (Korean red chile paste) and 1 teaspoon *doenjang* (Korean soybean paste) into some chicken stock in a saucepan. Bring to a boil and add your instant noodles along with whatever you have in your refrigerator (for me this is usually some combination of scallions, Chinese cabbage, seaweed, chopped red chiles, shrimp, shredded chicken, tofu, or egg), until noodles are cooked.

LIZZIE MABBOTT'S *RAMYUN*
Author of *Chinatown Kitchen*

Cook your instant noodles following the package directions along with the seasoning sachet. Fry some Spam chunks in a dry, nonstick skillet over medium heat until crisp, then add these to the drained noodles. Top with a soft-boiled egg and finish with a drizzle of ginger and scallion oil, along with a good shake of *shichimi togarashi* (Japanese spice mix).

JOE MCPHERSON'S *RAMYUN*
Founder of ZenKimchi.com

Boil your instant noodles in water (without the seasoning
sachet) and drain once cooked. Heat a little vegetable oil
in a pan and throw in the drained noodles along with the
seasoning from the *ramyun* package. Crack in an egg,
and scramble it in. Toss in some pasta sauce and mix in
until just heated through. My brother swears by this!

DA-HAE'S *RAMYUN*

2¼ cups water
2 to 3 bird's-eye chiles, finely sliced
1¾oz mature *Baechu Kimchi* (see page 32), drained and
    coarsely chopped
1¾oz pork belly, cut into matchsticks

1 x 4½oz package hot and spicy *Shin Ramyun*
    instant noodles
1 scallion, trimmed and finely sliced
1 egg

1_ Bring the measurement water to a boil in a saucepan
   along with the chiles, *kimchi*, and pork belly. Add the
   noodles, noodle seasoning sachet, and scallion and
   continue to cook for 2 minutes.

2_ Turn off the heat, make a well in the middle of the
   noodles with a chopstick or fork and crack in the egg.
   Pile the noodles carefully over the egg to cover, then
   put the lid on the pan and let stand for 2 minutes for
   the egg to poach. Serve immediately—the egg whites
   should be firm and the yolk perfectly poached.

GARETH'S *RAMYUN*

1 x 4½oz package hot and spicy *Shin Ramyun*
    instant noodles
1 bird's-eye chile, finely sliced
1 tablespoon vegetable oil

2½oz cooked chicken meat, shredded
1 processed cheese slice
1 tablespoon shredded medium Cheddar cheese
2 scallions, finely sliced

1_ Put the noodles in a saucepan with the chile, add enough boiling water to cover, and cook (without the seasoning sachet) for 1 to 2 minutes, until the noodles are al dente and just cooked. Drain and set aside.

2_ Heat the oil in a skillet over medium heat. Add the chicken and fry for 2 to 3 minutes until heated through. Add the drained noodles along with the seasoning from the noodle package and fry for

another minute, stirring everything together to make sure the noodles are evenly coated in the seasoning.

3_ Transfer the noodles to a large bowl and top with the processed and shredded cheeses. Cover with a plate and let stand for 2 minutes for the cheese to melt a little, then scatter with the scallions to serve.

08

Drinks & Drinking Culture

At the end of hardship comes

HAPPINESS

If you've ever been to Korea–or even seen the video for Psy's Hangover–you'll have some idea of what drinking in Korea is like. Drinking is an important part of Korean culture. Koreans see it as an important way of forming bonds and relationships, because drinking makes people let their guard down. In fact, there's even a saying which translates as, "One glass isn't enough, three's too little, five's the right number, and seven's pushing the limit." I've heard my uncle say this before and it's a rule I'm pretty sure he sticks to.

The most popular alcohol in Korea is *soju*, which was traditionally made by distilling rice and water. Nowadays, the mass-produced varieties contain a mixture of grains (including wheat, barley, and tapioca) along with ethanol, water, and sweeteners. It's cheap (and so is an easy way to get drunk); one bottle of standard 13fl oz, 19 percent ABV *soju* normally costs around ₩1,200 or about $1. *Soju* is a clear spirit, like vodka, but it tastes a little sweeter and feels smoother. It's usually served chilled and poured into shot glasses, though there's a real culture of mixing your drinks in Korea, which we'll go into more detail on later. As well as *soju*, other popular drinks include:

Makgeolli

Makgeolli is a fermented drink (some say rice wine, some say rice beer) made with rice using a Korean fermentation starter called nuruk. It's a creamy, cloudy drink that's slightly sweet and a little bit fizzy. It's about six percent ABV and is usually drunk from metal or wooden bowls. Traditionally favored by farmers and the elderly (it's often considered to be quite filling), *makgeolli* used to be a pretty unfashionable drink, though that's now changed with the rise of *makgeolli* bars, which sell different variations of it, including chestnut, *yuja* (yuzu), berry, and sesame.

Beer

Beer, or *mekju* as it's called in Korean, is very popular. The Korean brands OB, Cass, and Hite dominate the market with their light, easy-to-drink beer. People more used to Western-style beers often find Korean beer quite watery and weak, but because it's so light, it's makes a great accompaniment to Korean food, which is often full of strong flavors.

Bekseju

Bekseju or "one-hundred-year-old wine" refers to how old you might live to be when drinking it, thanks to its apparent health properties. *Bekseju* is made with Korean sweet (glutinous) rice and is flavored with ginseng and 11 other spices and herbs including ginger, cinnamon, and licorice, all of which combined are said to help you live a long life. It is a little sweet, and the predominant ginseng flavor can taste quite medicinal at first until you get used to it.

Sansachun

Sansachun is another drink known for its medicinal properties, and is said to help calm your nerves. Supposedly, a shot of this a day will keep the doctor away. *Sansachun* is made from the red berries of the *sansa* (hawthorn) and is very sweet and syrupy, so it's best enjoyed before a meal rather than with food.

Bokbunja

Bokbunja is a syrupy wine made with black raspberries that is usually between 15 to 19 percent ABV. It's sweet, mild, and deep red in color, and works really well with desserts. I like to pour it all over an Eton mess because the flavor really complements the berries and meringues. It's said to help promote "male stamina" (like a lot of things which are said to be good for the health in Korea), and so is a popular drink with honeymooners. The best thing about *bokbunja* though has to be its translation, which is "a force so strong, it could knock a urinal over," illustrating perfectly how easy to drink it is.

Maesilju

Maesilju is made from small green plums called *maesil*. It usually comes in a green bottle with a wide top and a few plums in the bottom. It's both sweet and tart since the plums are usually fermented with plenty of sugar, and it's usually drunk from small shot glasses like *soju*. However, it can also be enjoyed as a dessert wine or in cocktails.

DRINKING RULES

People new to Korean drinking culture are often surprised by how many rules there are. These rules include:

- Drink the drink you're given. It's considered very rude to refuse a drink—even if you're not a big drinker, you'd be expected to at least take the first glass.
- Make sure to pour and receive drinks with both hands, unless you're drinking with friends, or if you're the eldest.
- The first drink should be with everyone all together, so that you can say, "cheers" or *gumbae* in Korean.
- The youngest at the table should pour the drink, unless someone older takes it from them.
- Never fill your own glass, particularly if it's a sharing bottle such as *soju*. Always keep an eye on everyone else's glasses to be ready to pour them a drink so that their glass doesn't sit empty. Koreans also believe that you shouldn't top off a glass that is half-full (you should wait until that person has drained their shot).

HWESHIK

Most companies in Korea will take part in something called *hweshik*, which translates as "company dinner," since it combines the words *hwesa* (company) and *shiksa* (meal). These company meals are held on a regular basis (once or twice a month) and are pretty mandatory if you want to get anywhere in business. *Hweshik* is more than just eating together and is very different to the average company get-together in the UK, for example, since it's actually an event that takes place in several rounds called *il cha*, *ee cha*, *sam cha*, *sa cha* (and if you're still standing, *o cha*)—rounds one, two, three, four, and five, with each round taking place in a different location.

Il Cha (1)

Hweshiks usually kick off at a Korean BBQ restaurant, with the boss ordering meat (usually *samgyeopsal*, see page 92) for the entire table along with plenty of drink (usually beer and *soju*).

Ee Cha (2)

After the barbecue, the next place is the pub, or *hof* as it's called in Korean. This will include more food called *anju* (usually Korean Fried Chicken, see page 212) and a few bottles of *soju* will be ordered.

Sam Cha (3)

Sam cha is often another *hof* for a change of scenery and plenty more drinks. At this point, there will be a lot more drinking games going on.

Sa Cha (4)

For round four, everyone then moves over to the *noraebang* or karaoke. Karaokes can be found all over Korea and are usually private rooms with a big screen, a fat book of songs to choose from, and a few tambourines. It doesn't matter if you don't have the best voice because the whole thing is more about the bonding experience. However, to "save face," some people (members of my family included) practice four to five songs to make sure they're able to belt them out perfectly when their time comes.

O Cha (5)

If you have the stamina to last until *o cha* (impressive), then it's time to move to a club for more drinks and lots of dancing, often until the sun starts to rise . . .

MIXING DRINKS

Mixing your drinks is very common in Korea, with "bomb" type drinks being particularly popular, and not just reserved for university students. Even when President Lee Myung Bak was in office, he'd always drink *soju* bombs when he was drinking in public with other high-ranking officials.

Somek

The most popular *soju* mix is *somek*—a glass of beer mixed with *soju*. You put a glass of *soju* at the bottom of a beer glass, pour beer up to the rim, and stick a chopstick in the center which you then hit hard with the other chopstick to cause bubbles to rise and mix everything together. Another way to mix a *somek* is to line up a row of beers with shots of *soju* balanced in between them to create a *soju* train. The first *soju* shot is then flicked over so that all the *soju* glasses fall into the beer in a domino effect.

Go-jin-gam-rae

Translating as "no pain, no gain," this drink is a combination of cola, *soju*, and beer. Place a shot glass three-quarters full of cola at the bottom of a beer glass followed by an empty shot glass on top, which you fill with *soju*. Beer is then poured in the gap next to the glasses until it reaches the top, with the idea being to drink this all in one (or "one shot" as Koreans say) so that you get the fizz of the beer, followed by the *soju*, and then finish with the sweetness of cola.

O-Sip-Se-Ju

Bekseju or "one-hundred-year-old wine" becomes *o-sip-se-ju* or "fifty-year-old wine" when mixed in equal quantities of *soju*.

So-baek-san-mek

This drink is named after the initials of all the component drinks and is a simple mix of equal parts of *soju*, *bekseju*, *sansachun*, and *mekju* (beer). This is often mixed by the bottle into a pitcher.

HANGOVER CURES

Due to having such a big drinking culture, Korea has a *lot* of hangover cures. The most popular include soups, such as *Gamjatang* (see page 157), beansprout soup, *haejangguk* (which literally translates as "hangover cure soup"), and dried pollack soup.

There are also lots of different energy drinks that you can buy at a corner store (or pharmacy if you're in need of something stronger) in small brown or green bottles. You down these in one shot to get rid of a hangover. One of the most popular is called Condition; you drink one before you start consuming any alcohol and then drink another one the next day. Most Koreans will swear that you won't feel a thing, no matter how much you've had to drink the night before.

DRINKING GAMES

Gareth has been introduced to a whole host of different drinking games by my cousins, which include the following:

Flicking the Soju Cap

The common green *soju* bottles have a metal screwtop lid. As you open the bottle, you're often left with a metal thread dangling from the side, which you twist in on itself to create a little stick. Everyone around the table has a turn flicking the stick. The winner is the person who is able to get the stick to fly off and the person before them has to drink a shot.

Baskin Robbins 31

I'm not sure why this is called Baskin Robbins, but basically everyone around the table counts up to three numbers in order. For example: one or one, two or one, two, three. This goes around the group until it gets to 30. Whoever 31 lands on must drink.

Three, Six, Nine

Go around the table and count in order starting from one. Any time a number has a three, six, or nine in it, the person has to clap, until the numbers reach double figures (33, 36, 39), in which case you have to clap twice. Whoever says the wrong number or claps in the wrong place (or forgets to clap twice) has to drink a shot.

Titanic

Fill a glass with beer and then float an empty shot glass on top. Everyone has a turn pouring a little bit of alcohol into the shot glass and whoever makes it sink has to drink.

Everyone Drinks

Each person takes turns to get everyone else around the table to have a drink by coming up with criteria for those who have to take a shot. For example, "all the people wearing jeans, drink," or "all the men over 20, drink." This game is fast-paced and dangerous because it's so open to stitching someone up.

The Black Knight/Rose

If you've reached a point in your evening where you really can't drink anymore, you can nominate a Black Knight (for men) or Black Rose (for women) as someone to take your drink for you. By doing this though, your ball is very much in the Black Knight or Rose's court because they can think up the terms of repayment (a favor or dare) and then there's always the risk that they might refuse you, in which case you have to drink two shots instead. It's a pretty risky business and only really suggested for desperate times!

Kimchi Bloody Mary

In Korea, eating and drinking with your colleagues (and boss) is an important part of team bonding called *hweshik*. This midweek drinking culture means that hangovers can be a common problem, which explains Korea's many different hangover cures. Here we've taken the traditional Bloody Mary recipe but given it a bit of an extra Korean chile kick with the *kimchi* and *gochugaru*. We've also decorated this drink with beansprouts as a cheeky nod to the (many) Korean hangover soups in which they feature.

SERVES 1

1 long red chile, trimmed, seeded, and finely chopped
ice cubes
1¼fl oz vodka
1fl oz *soju* (Korean rice/grain spirit)
3 tablespoons juice drained from *kimchi*

¼ cup tomato juice
2 teaspoons lime juice
½ teaspoon Worcestershire sauce

TO DECORATE
1 tablespoon *gochugaru* (Korean red chile powder)
¼ lime
3 to 4 beansprouts
1 stalk celery

1_ Put the chile at the bottom of a beer glass and squash it with the end of a rolling pin (or muddler if you have one) to release its flavor.

2_ Fill the glass with ice cubes, then add the vodka, *soju*, *kimchi* juice, tomato juice, lime juice, and Worcestershire sauce. Pour the cocktail into a second beer glass, then return it to the original glass. Repeat the process 3 times (the aim is to chill the cocktail without melting the ice and diluting the drink).

3_ Spread the *gochugaru* evenly over a small plate. Run the lime quarter along the rim of a highball glass, then dip the rim of the glass in the *gochugaru* to coat. Fill the glass with ice cubes, strain over the cocktail mix, and decorate with a few beansprouts and a celery stalk to serve.

Apple and Chile Smash

When I order something from a menu that says it has chile in it, I really want to be able to feel that chile heat. Now, I don't necessarily mean I want my head blown off, but I definitely want to know that there's some chile in there. That's why I love this drink, in which the sour apple contrasts with the chile's prickly, fruity heat. It'll leave your tongue tingling.

½ lime, cut into quarters
½ apple, cut into ½-inch cubes
1 red chile, trimmed, seeded, and coarsely chopped
2 teaspoons superfine sugar

2fl oz apple vodka
crushed ice
2fl oz clear lemonade
1 red bird's-eye chile, to decorate

1_ Put the lime, apple, chopped chile, and sugar in a pitcher. Using the end of a rolling pin (or a cocktail muddler if you have one), squash the ingredients together to let their flavors infuse.

2_ Pour the apple vodka into a highball glass and fill with crushed ice. Add the smashed lime and apple mixture to the glass and stir together well with a cocktail spoon. Add the lemonade.

3_ Cut a slit in the middle of the bird's-eye chile, prop it on the rim of the glass to decorate, and serve.

Grown-up Yakult

Ever since I was little, I've been kind of addicted to Yakult. The milky probiotic always reminds me of Korea (I drank at least three to four bottles a day when I was there). Even now my aunt always has some in her fridge ready for me when I visit because she knows how much I love it. Combining it with *soju* might sound a little peculiar, but along with the soda, this cocktail actually ends up tasting like fizzy candy. Trust me.

SERVES
1

ice cubes
2½fl oz *soju* (Korean rice/grain spirit)
1 Yakult (2¼fl oz)
2½fl oz lemon-flavored fizzy soft drink, such as 7Up or Sprite

Fill a highball glass with ice cubes. Pour in the *soju*,
Yakult, and the lemon-flavored soft drink to finish.
Stir together with a cocktail spoon and serve.

Soju Mule

This cocktail was the most popular drink at our first ever popup in Tooting market, in southwest London. It is almost sinfully simple but the sweetness of the *soju* contrasts brilliantly with the sourness of the lime and the bitterness of the Angostura. This drink is amazing served in a huge pitcher filled with ice for friends to share on a summer's day.

SERVES
1

ice cubes
1 lime, cut into eighths
10 drops of Angostura bitters

2½fl oz *soju* (Korean rice/grain spirit)
2¾fl oz ginger beer

1_ Fill a highball glass with ice cubes.

2_ Squeeze the lime segments over the ice, then drop
the rinds into the glass. Add the Angostura bitters,
soju, and ginger beer. Stir together with a cocktail
spoon and serve.

Baesuk Martini

Definitely one for those with a sweet tooth, *Baesuk* is a traditional Korean punch made from steamed pear, cinnamon, honey, and *jujube*. Here these flavors combine perfectly with rum to create a lightly spiced martini version of this Korean sweet treat.

SERVES 1

14oz can of pears in syrup
1 cinnamon stick
1 tablespoon liquid honey
ice cubes

½fl oz spiced light rum
1¼fl oz vodka
1 *jujube* (dried red dates), to decorate (optional)

1_ Drain the syrup from the pears into a saucepan and set the pears to one side.

2_ Add the cinnamon stick and honey to the pan and heat gently for 2 to 3 minutes, stirring, until the honey has dissolved. Remove from the heat and set aside for 5 minutes to allow the flavors to infuse, then remove the cinnamon stick and let stand for another 5 minutes to cool.

3_ Fill a martini glass with ice cubes to chill, then discard the ice.

4_ Fill a beer glass with ice cubes. Add the rum, vodka, and 2fl oz of the cooled syrup and gently stir the ingredients together with a cocktail spoon.

5_ Place the *jujube* at the bottom of the martini glass and strain the cocktail mix over it.

195

HongCho Collins

HongCho is a flavored drinking vinegar with added fruit concentrate. In Korea, it's usually enjoyed in the summer, mixed with sparkling water and poured over ice, as a tangy, refreshing drink. This cocktail mixes HongCho with *soju*—the tang of the drinking vinegar taking away the harsh alcoholic edge of the spirit. Dangerously delicious, it's perhaps a little too easy to drink.

SERVES
1

ice cubes
2½fl oz *soju* (Korean rice/grain spirit)
2½fl oz pomegranate HongCho
1fl oz lemon juice
1¼fl oz *bokbunja* (Korean berry wine)

1fl oz sugar syrup
soda water, to top off

TO DECORATE
slice of lemon
1 tablespoon pomegranate seeds

1_ Fill a highball glass with ice cubes and set aside.

2_ Fill a cocktail shaker with ice cubes. Add the *soju*, HongCho, lemon juice, *bokbunja*, and sugar syrup and shake vigorously for about 1 minute, or until a frost forms on the side of the shaker.

3_ Strain the cocktail into the highball glass and top off with soda water. Decorate with a slice of lemon and some pomegranate seeds.

TIP: Make your own sugar syrup by stirring together equal parts superfine sugar and water until the sugar has dissolved.

Anju & Bar Snacks

09

STARTING
IS Half the JOB

In Korea it is very difficult to go for a drink without food. The very fact that Korean has a specific word, anju, to describe the food that you eat when drinking shows how the two are linked and (outside of westernized districts) Korean hofs or pubs will expect you to order something to eat whenever you order any drinks. This is partly because the alcohol is generally very cheap, but also because drinking is a sociable experience best enjoyed in a group with plenty of food to share. Plus, it's never a bad idea to line your stomach when drinking.

The recipes we've included here are the messy kind of fast-food style *anju* that we love. They're mostly designed for sharing and are perfect with a few shots of *soju* or beer.

READING AN *ANJU* MENU

When you arrive at a *hof* you are usually given a menu which is split into several categories of *anju*:

Chicken

Korean fried chicken is the ultimate *anju* for us. Double-fried, super-crispy, juicy chicken is the perfect accompaniment to an ice-cold beer. It's usually available plain, with either sweet-and-spicy or soy glazes, or with piles of minced garlic on top. The chicken is usually served with two forks per person, so you can pull the meat apart without getting your fingers too dirty, and with a side of pickled mooli to help cleanse the palate between bites.

Soups and Stews

Soups and stews eaten as *anju* are usually quite spicy or salty because that pairs well with most Korean alcohol, which acts as a palate cleanser. Examples include beansprout soup (some people believe that it prevents a hangover if they eat it while they're drinking), *kimchi jjigae*, and *ramyun*.

Deep-fried

Deep-fried *anju* are somewhat varied and can include tempuras, fries, and even potato smiley faces. Gareth and my dad have ordered "assorted fried potato" from a *hof* before, thinking that they might receive a plate of french fries, but what they were actually given was a mixture of hash browns, french fries, smiley faces, and deep-fried balls of mashed potatoes.

Dried

Dried *anju* are the ones we'd normally go for on days when we're feeling really, really full. Dried *anju* are usually a choice of dried or partially dried squid (accompanied by ketchup and mayo for dipping), dried and sweetened filefish (a type of tropical fish), dried anchovies and/or nuts. These are often served with peanut M&M's®.

Fruit

For those wanting a healthier or lighter option, you can always order a platter of fruit, or one of fruit and ham. These platters tend to be quite expensive, usually a similar price to a plate of fried chicken, which is why we never end up ordering them.

Traditional

Other than the soups and stews, traditional *anju* include *dubu kimchi* (steamed tofu with *kimchi* and fried pork), steamed silkworm *pupae* (not a favorite of ours), and *pajeon* (scallion pancakes).

Spoon Pizza

Gareth and I had spoon pizza on our first trip to Korea together. We'd ordered it more out of curiosity than anything else at one of the pubs we visited with my cousin Jisoo. I can't remember what the toppings were on that first one we got, but the idea of eating pizza with a spoon stuck in our heads. Spoon pizza is about the best bit of the pizza—the cheesy, tomatoey, gooey topping—with the tortilla wrap acting simply as something for your spoon to scrape against as you dig into the pan. I can imagine lots of Italians looking at this recipe and shaking their heads in despair, but it really is the perfect dish to be shared with friends, armed with a few spoons and lots of drinks.

SERVES
4

2 flour tortilla wraps, cut into quarters
¼ cup *Gochujang* Ketchup (see page 80)
½ cup medium Cheddar cheese, shredded
½ cup red Leicester cheese, shredded

1¾oz soft mozzarella cheese
1¾oz *nduja* (hot Italian sausage paste)
2 tablespoons Really Great Cheese Sauce (see page 82)

1_ Preheat the oven to 400°F.

2_ Lay half the tortilla quarters flat in a cast-iron ridged grill pan, with the curved edges on the outside to form a circle. Lay the remaining tortilla quarters over the top so that they overlap, ensuring the bottom of the pan is completely covered.

3_ Smear the *gochujang* ketchup all over the tortillas, making sure they are completely covered, then sprinkle with the shredded cheeses. Tear the mozzarella into small pieces and dot them over the surface of the pizza along with the '*nduja*, then spoon small amounts of the cheese sauce evenly all over it.

4_ Put the pan in the oven and bake for 15 minutes until all the cheese has completely melted and is gooey. Serve immediately. If you have a fondue set, place the pan on the stand over the flame to keep the cheese soft and melted.

TIP: The topping here can be anything you like. I'm pretty sure we've had chicken and pepperoni on spoon pizzas before, so feel free to get creative and add any of your favorite pizza topping ingredients.

Gochu Twiguim CHILES STUFFED WITH SPAM AND CHEESE

Whenever I see any kind of stuffed, fried chile on a menu, I have to have it. And if I ever saw this version on a menu, I'd be ordering it by the bucket-load. In Korea, fried chiles are both a common street food and *anju*, but they're usually filled with a *mandu*-style filling of ground pork. In this one, I've combined my love for the light, Korean-style batter, with my loves for cheese and Spam. The result is crispy, spicy chiles filled with oozy, melting cheese with a meaty, salty bite from the Spam. Delicious.

MAKES 10

10 long green chiles
2½oz Spam, finely diced
½ onion, finely diced
½ bird's-eye chile, trimmed and finely sliced
9oz soft mozzarella cheese

vegetable oil, for frying

BATTER
1¼ cups all-purpose flour
½ teaspoon baking powder
½ teaspoon garlic granules

½ teaspoon freshly ground black pepper
½ teaspoon salt
2 eggs

1_ For the batter, mix together the dry ingredients in a bowl. In a separate bowl, beat together the eggs. Set aside.

2_ Using a sharp knife, make a cut down the middle of each long green chile to create an opening, being careful not to go right through the other side. Remove the seeds and membranes.

3_ Heat a splash of vegetable oil in a skillet over medium heat, then add the Spam, onion, and bird's-eye chile. Cook, stirring, for 4 to 5 minutes until the onions have softened and the Spam begins to brown and crisp at the edges.

4_ Add the Spam, onion, and chile to a large bowl, tear over the mozzarella, add the salt, and mix everything together with a wooden spoon. Spoon a tablespoon or so of the Spam and mozzarella mixture into each chile, being careful to fill them completely but not overstuff them. Press the chiles back together to seal the filling in.

5_ Half-fill a large pot or deep-fryer with vegetable oil and heat to 350°F, or until a cube of bread dropped in the oil browns in 30 seconds.

6_ Dip a stuffed chile into the beaten egg, moving it around with your fingertips to make sure it is completely coated, then dip it into the flour mixture. Lightly toss the flour all over the chile to ensure it is fully coated on all sides, then carefully shake off any excess flour. Repeat with the remaining chiles.

7_ Lower the stuffed chiles carefully into the hot oil and fry for 2 to 3 minutes until golden. Remove from the fryer and shake off the excess oil, then let drain and cool for 2 minutes on paper towels before serving. Be careful because they will be molten hot inside!

K-fries

Dripping in cheese, sour cream, *kimchi*, and the meaty juices from the ground beef, Korean fries, or K-fries, are unapologetically messy. An American-Korean fusion food, they've been really big in the USA (particularly LA) for quite some time now thanks to the likes of Roy Choi and his hugely popular Kogi taco trucks. They have also started to make their way over to Korea too and we've noticed several different variations of them on our last few visits. Just make sure you've got plenty of napkins before attempting to eat them!

SERVES
2

14oz oven-ready regular fries
vegetable oil, for frying
3½oz ground beef
3 tablespoons *Bulgogi* Sauce (see page 95)
¾ cup medium Cheddar cheese, shredded

3½oz *Baechu Kimchi* (see page 32), drained and
 coarsely chopped
1 long red pickled chile, pickled overnight in Simple
 Pickle Brine (see page 82) and finely chopped

2 scallions, trimmed and finely sliced, plus extra
 to garnish
2 tablespoons sour cream

1_ Cook the fries following the package directions.

2_ Heat a splash of vegetable oil in a skillet over medium heat, add the ground beef, and fry for 3 to 4 minutes until browned. Then add the *bulgogi* sauce and cook for another 2 minutes until the sauce has thickened and reduced. Set aside.

3_ Once cooked, remove the fries from the oven and place them in a baking dish. Sprinkle one-quarter of the cheese over the fries, then spoon the *bulgogi* and ground beef mixture evenly over the top. Scatter with the *kimchi*, red chile, scallions, and the rest of the cheese, then place the fries under a hot broiler for 2 minutes, until the cheese is bubbling and melted.

4_ Dollop the sour cream generously over the fries, scatter with scallions, and serve immediately.

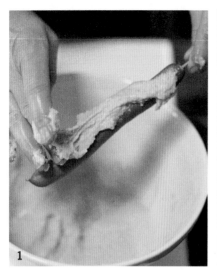

Gamja Wiener SHOESTRING FRIES ON A STICK

These seem to be sold at almost every street food stand in Korea. Deep-fried wieners coated in a cornmeal batter with fat fries stuck all over them, they look amazing. However, the fries combined with the cornmeal batter can make them stodgy. Still, we really wanted to bring a version back home because we thought they had the potential to be great. After testing the recipe a few times, we discovered that shoestring fries were the way forward because they go really crisp in the fryer, giving you a crunchy outside with a soft cornmeal-battered wiener in the middle. Squeeze lots of ketchup and mustard onto them for a truly authentic experience.

4 baking potatoes, peeled
vegetable oil, for deep-frying
4 large wieners

4 bamboo skewers, soaked in water for at least 10 minutes

BATTER
1 cup all-purpose flour
1 cup cornmeal
2 teaspoons baking powder
1 tablespoon superfine sugar
pinch of salt

²/₃ cup milk
1 egg

TO SERVE
Gochujang Ketchup (see page 80)
mustard

1_ Cut the potatoes into ultrathin sticks using a mandoline or julienne peeler. Put the potato pieces in a colander and rinse under cold running water, then place in a large bowl with enough water to cover. Let stand for 10 minutes to draw out the excess starch.

2_ Meanwhile, put all the batter ingredients in a large bowl and mix together well. Set aside. Half-fill a large pot or deep-fryer with vegetable oil and heat to 350°F, or until a cube of bread dropped in the oil browns in 30 seconds.

3_ Drain the potatoes and pat dry with paper towels, then lower them carefully into the hot oil. Fry for 10 seconds, then remove from the oil and drain on a platter lined with paper towels. Arrange the fries in an even layer, all roughly pointing in the same direction.

4_ Thread a bamboo skewer through the length of each wiener. Dip the wiener skewers in the batter one at a time, then cover with extra batter to make sure they are completely coated. Lay one of the wiener skewers on top of the shoestring fries and gently roll it until coated all over, patting the fries into the batter. Repeat with the remaining skewers.

5_ Carefully lower the wiener skewers into the hot oil and fry for 2 to 3 minutes, or until the batter is crisp and golden brown. Drain on paper towels and serve with *gochujang* ketchup and mustard.

SERVES
4

Kimchi Mac 'n' Cheese

There's something about putting *kimchi* and cheese together that just works because the tangy *kimchi* lifts the thick cheese sauce and gives it a bit of a chile kick. Combined with the crunchy, salty bread crumbs, this dish is pure comfort food. We've served this as a side dish at our popups before, alongside our pork belly buns (see page 108), but this macaroni and cheese dish is also great on its own.

SERVES 4

1 cup Really Great Cheese Sauce (see page 82)
11½oz dried elbow macaroni
2 tablespoons matured *Baechu Kimchi* (see page 32)
2 scallions, trimmed and finely sliced

TOPPING
5½oz matured *Baechu Kimchi* (see page 32), drained and cut into ½-inch pieces
3 slices smoked bacon

½ tablespoon *gochugaru* (Korean red chile powder)
1 small whole garlic clove
1½ cups fresh bread crumbs

1_ For the topping, lay the *kimchi* pieces out flat on a large baking pan. Put the pan in the oven on its lowest setting and let the *kimchi* dry out for about 6 hours until it is crispy. Set aside.

2_ Put the bacon in a dry skillet over medium heat and fry for 3 to 4 minutes, until the edges start to turn crisp and the bacon is cooked through. Add to a blender along with the dried *kimchi*, *gochugaru*, and garlic and pulse until everything is finely chopped. Return the pan to the heat, add the bread crumbs, and let them toast, stirring, for 4 to 5 minutes until the bread crumbs are completely dry. Add to the other topping ingredients and set aside.

3_ Warm the cheese sauce over medium heat, stirring it occasionally and adding some extra milk if it is too thick. Set aside.

4_ Meanwhile, bring a pan of salted water to a boil, add the macaroni, and cook following the package directions until al dente. Drain and return to the pan, then mix in the cheese sauce, *kimchi*, and scallions. Spoon into bowls and scatter with a handful of the crispy topping to finish.

TIP: If you have one, place the *kimchi* topping pieces in a dehydrator rather than the oven to get them really dried out and crunchy.

Korean Fried Chicken

Double-fried, so the coating gets really crunchy but the meat stays juicy and really tender, Korean fried chicken really is the best kind of fried chicken there is. On a recent trip to Korea with some friends—and despite spending our days sampling all the street food that Korea has to offer, followed by evenings of Korean BBQ——we'd end our nights at a pub with a big plateful of the stuff. Well, you have to order *anju* in a pub and the chicken was always too hard to resist, no matter how full we were. Nothing goes better with an ice-cold beer.

SERVES **4**

2¼lb chicken wings
2 pints *Kimchi* Brine (see page 94)
vegetable oil, for deep-frying
3 eggs
½ quantity Korean Sweet Chile Sauce (see page 86),
    for brushing

COATING
1 cup potato starch
⅓ cup sweet rice flour
⅔ cup all-purpose flour
1 tablespoon baking powder
½ tablespoon salt

1_ Put the chicken wings in a large bowl and add the brine. Transfer to the refrigerator and let stand for 1 hour.

2_ After 1 hour, drain the chicken wings and rinse them under cold running water to remove the excess salt from the brine, then pat dry with paper towels.

3_ Half-fill a large pot or deep-fryer with vegetable oil and heat to 350°F, or until a cube of bread dropped in the oil browns in 30 seconds.

4_ Put the chicken in a large bowl. Crack the eggs over the top and rub in using your hands. In a separate bowl, mix together the coating ingredients. Pour the mixture onto the chicken wings and massage with your hands until evenly coated.

5_ Shake the chicken wings gently to remove any excess coating, then carefully lower into the hot oil. Fry for 4 to 5 minutes until the chicken begins to color.

6_ Lift the chicken out of the oil for 4 to 5 minutes (this will allow the oil to get back up to temperature as well as give the chicken a moment to rest), then carefully lower the chicken back into the oil and fry for another 3 minutes until golden.

7_ Drain the chicken on paper towels, brush with a little chile sauce, and serve immediately with plenty of napkins.

Garlicky Gizzards

I don't know many people who ate chickens' gizzards growing up, but I've always been a fan. We spent many summer vacations in Spain, and my mom would often pick up a pack of chicken gizzards from the local supermarket. She'd bring them back to the house and quickly sauté them with fresh chile, garlic, and salt. Cooked quickly like this, the gizzards are quite chewy (which I like). Gareth has never been too convinced by the texture, so we found that brining the gizzards first and trimming them of any sinew makes them much more tender, while still retaining their flavor. We've added a little bit of chicken liver here too to balance out the texture.

SERVES 2

7oz chicken gizzards, cleaned and trimmed of any sinew
2 pints *Kimchi* Brine (see page 94)
1½ tablespoons vegetable oil, divided
1¾oz chicken livers, cleaned, trimmed of any sinew, and cut into thin strips

1 teaspoon butter
1 long red chile, trimmed, seeded, and finely sliced
2 garlic cloves, finely sliced
pinch of salt
pinch of pepper

1 tablespoon *soju* (Korean rice/grain spirit) or sake
½ scallion, trimmed and finely sliced, to garnish

1_ Put the gizzards in a large bowl and add the brine. Transfer to the refrigerator and let stand for 1 hour.

2_ After 1 hour, drain the gizzards and rinse them under cold running water to remove the excess salt from the brine, then pat dry with paper towels.

3_ Heat 1 tablespoon of the vegetable oil in a large skillet over high heat. Add the chicken liver and fry, stirring, for 30 seconds, then add ½ teaspoon of butter to the pan. Once the butter has melted, add the liver to a bowl and set aside.

4_ Return the pan to the heat and add the remaining ½ tablespoon of oil. Reduce the heat to medium, add the gizzards, chile, garlic, salt, and pepper and fry for 2 to 3 minutes until the gizzards are cooked through. Add the *soju*, liver, and remaining butter to the skillet and fry another 30 seconds. Transfer to a plate and serve garnished with the scallion.

TIP: These gizzards also make a great appetizer. Toast a couple of slices of rye or sourdough bread in the skillet after cooking to soak up the juices, then top with the gizzard mixture to finish.

Chorizo and Kimchi Hash

With its winning combination of smoky chorizo, tangy *kimchi,* and runny eggs, this hash is the ultimate brunch food, although it's just as good shared as an *anju* to help soak up all that beer.

1lb 2oz new potatoes
1 tablespoon vegetable oil
1 red onion, finely sliced
1¾oz dried chorizo sausage, finely chopped
100g *Baechu Kimchi* (see page 32), drained

5 cherry tomatoes, halved
1 garlic clove, minced
2 eggs
salt
buttered crusty bread slices, to serve

TO GARNISH
1 scallion, trimmed and finely chopped
1 teaspoon *gochugaru* (Korean red chile powder)

1_ Bring a large saucepan of salted water to a boil, add the potatoes, and cook for 15 minutes, until tender. Drain and rinse under cold water and cut into bite-sized chunks.

2_ Heat the oil in a cast-iron ridged grill pan. Fry the onion and chorizo for 2 to 3 minutes, until the onion has just softened. Add the *kimchi*, tomatoes, and garlic and fry for another minute, then add the potatoes. Cook, stirring gently, for another 2 minutes.

3_ Make two wells in the center of the hash with a spoon and crack an egg into each. Place the pan under a hot broiler for 3 to 4 minutes, or until the whites of the eggs are cooked through but the yolks are still runny.

4_ Garnish with scallion and *gochugaru* and serve immediately with thick slices of crusty buttered bread.

Lotus Root Nachos

Sweet, salty, and irresistible, these crispy nachos are a twist on the traditional and make the perfect party snack. They require minimum effort, while the pretty pattern of the sliced lotus roots looks seriously impressive. Lotus roots are traditionally served as *banchan*, often braised in soy sauce. Though they look attractive, I never think they taste that great, and I much prefer eating them like this.

4 lotus roots, about 7oz each, trimmed
juice of 1 lemon
vegetable oil, for deep-frying

SEASONING
1 teaspoon salt

1 teaspoon sesame oil
1 tablespoon garlic granules
1½ teaspoons superfine sugar
1 tablespoon *gochugaru* (Korean red chile powder)
1 tablespoon paprika

TO SERVE
Zingy Green Sauce (see page 79)
Kimchi Salsa (see page 79)

1_ Using a sharp knife or a mandoline, cut the lotus root widthwise into ⅛-inch slices. Place the lotus root slices in a bowl, covering them with the lemon juice as you go to prevent them from turning brown.

2_ Half-fill a large pot or deep-fryer with vegetable oil and heat to 350°F, or until a cube of bread dropped in the oil browns in 30 seconds. Lower the lotus root slices carefully into the hot oil a few at a time (to stop them from sticking to one another). Fry for 3 minutes, or until the slices are crisp and slightly browned.

Shake off any excess oil and let drain on paper towels while repeating with the remaining slices.

3_ Meanwhile, mix together all the seasoning ingredients in a small bowl. Add the lotus root slices to a large bowl and sprinkle with the seasoning mixture a pinch at a time to prevent the mixture from clumping together. Toss the lotus root slices until they are thoroughly coated in the seasoning, then serve with zingy green sauce and *kimchi* salsa.

10

Sweet Treats

A SHIP WILL GO TO THE MOUNTAIN
IF THERE ARE TOO MANY CAPTAINS

Traditionally, Korea's never had that much in the way of desserts. Korean food is served all at the same time rather than as different courses, so Korean restaurants rarely have any sort of dessert offering and fruit is usually eaten at the end of the meal instead.

There are a couple of sweet treats that are famous in Korea such as *hotteok*, the chewy, crispy pancakes filled with caramel, and *bingsu*, a snowy, shaved ice that's eaten in the summer, but even these aren't usually served at the end the meal. *Hotteok* is a popular street food and *bingsu* is usually sold in cafes, separate from where you'd eat your main meal.

Even for special occasions, when sweet treats do sometimes make an appearance, they are usually in the form of cookies or ricecakes called *tteok*. *Tteok* are a chewier, stickier version of the Japanese *mochi* ricecakes. These are often filled with sweetened red bean paste or sugar and sesame seeds and are usually eaten during *Chusok* (Korean Thanksgiving).

Ricecakes don't really feel like a dessert to me though, and because desserts aren't really a big thing in Korea, we've always come up with Western-style desserts that incorporate Korean flavors for our popups and events. These include our *Yuja* Cheesecake (see page 220) and our Blueberry *Mandu* (see page 227), a variation on the sweet Polish *pierogi* (dumpling).

Korea does have a lot of bakeries, though. In fact, in the bigger cities, such as Seoul and Busan, it's difficult to walk down a street without passing one. These bakeries are often part of big chains that all sell similar breads and cakes. Some of the offerings are often a little unusual (think hotdog doughnuts, or tuna sandwiches on sugary, sweet bread), while others are more typically like cakes, such as *Soborro*, a bread with crisp topping made with peanuts, which we've based our cake recipe on (see page 224).

I think that many of the reasons why people like certain desserts are because of nostalgia, and this is also probably why I like *Soborro* so much. It's my go-to sweet treat whenever I visit a Korean bakery. Nostalgia is also the reason we had to include a recipe for banana milk in this chapter. You might say that banana milk isn't much of a dessert, but our version is thick, creamy, and full of ice cream, so it makes a great finish to a meal.

Yuja Cheesecake

For our first popup, we had to think really hard about a suitable dessert, since Korea isn't particularly known for its sweet treats. After playing around with a few ideas, we decided on this *yuja* cheesecake. *Yuja* is the Korean word for yuzu, a citrus fruit that has the zesty freshness of a lemon but with a slightly bitter edge. Here it combines perfectly with the rich cream cheese, to create a tangy, sweet dessert.

SERVES
8 to 10

1 cup heavy cream	**CRUST**	**TOPPING**
1½ cups cream cheese	3¼oz ginger snap cookies	1 cup *Yuja* Curd (see page 222)
½ superfine sugar	¾ cup graham cracker crumbs	2 tablespoons *yuja* (yuzu) juice
¼ cup *yuja* (yuzu) juice	⅔ stick butter, melted	½ teaspoon gelatin powder

1_ For the crust, break the cookies into a food processor, and add the graham cracker crumbs. Blend to a fine powder and pour into a bowl. Add the melted butter and stir until the mixture resembles wet sand.

2_ Spread the mixture into the bottom of an 8-inch springform cake pan, pressing it down with the back of a spoon to create an even layer. Transfer to the freezer for 5 minutes to set.

3_ Meanwhile, pour the heavy cream into a mixing bowl and beat to form stiff peaks. Add the cream cheese, sugar, and *yuja* juice and beat everything together.

4_ Remove the pan from the freezer and spread the cream cheese mixture evenly over the crust. Transfer to the refrigerator and let chill for at least 4 hours.

5_ Once the filling has set, make the topping. Gently heat the *yuja* curd and juice in a small saucepan over medium heat but do not let the mixture boil. Once the curd mixture is hot, add the gelatin powder. Stir continuously over the heat for 10 to 12 minutes, or until all the gelatin has dissolved into the liquid. Remove from the heat and set aside to cool.

6_ When the topping reaches room temperature, remove the cheesecake from the refrigerator and pour the cooled topping evenly over the surface. Return the cheesecake to the refrigerator and let set overnight before serving the following day.

Yuja Curd

This zesty, tangy, sweet curd has so many uses. Lemon curd has always been one of my favorite toast toppings, but *yuja* curd feels more like a special treat. Stir it into yogurt for breakfast, use it as a topping on desserts, or simply spread it on toast for a simple, delicious, and easy snack.

MAKES
1
SMALL JAR

2 eggs, plus 2 extra yolks
1 stick butter
1 cup superfine sugar

⅓ cup *yuja* (yuzu) juice
zest of 2 lemons

1_ Lightly beat the whole eggs and egg yolks together in a bowl.

2_ Melt the butter in a saucepan over medium heat, then add the sugar and mix together with a wooden spoon. Stir in the *yuja* juice and lemon zest, then add the eggs and continue to cook, stirring, for 8 to 10 minutes, or until the mixture is creamy and thick enough to coat the back of a spoon.

3_ Remove the pan from the heat. Once the curd has cooled, pour it into a sterilized jar and seal it. Store it in the refrigerator until ready to use. This will keep for up to a month unopened but use within a week once the jar has been opened.

Bingsu SUMMER SNOW

There is nothing better than *bingsu* in the summer. Made from shaved or crushed frozen milk, it cools you down much faster than eating ice cream and it's so light and refreshing. *Bingsu* can be topped with any fruit you like. On our most recent trip to Korea, I got hooked on a "mango cheese" version. It sounds weird, but essentially it tasted like mango cheesecake ice cream. Canned fruit works well here because the fruit is always soft enough to break apart with your spoon.

SERVES 4

2½ cups milk
1 x 15oz can mango slices, drained
vanilla ice cream, to serve

"CHEESECAKE" MIXTURE
3 tablespoons cream cheese
¼ cup heavy cream
2 tablespoons confectioner's sugar

1_ Pour the milk into ice cube trays and place them in the freezer for 3 to 4 hours, or until just set. (Don't allow the ice cubes to set too solidly or they will not break down properly in the food processor.)

2_ Meanwhile, mix together all the "cheesecake" ingredients in a small bowl. Set aside.

3_ Once the milky ice cubes have just frozen, add them to a food processor and pulse briefly together until the icy mixture resembles snow, but it shouldn't become too wet, like a slushie.

4_ Pour the ice mixture into a large bowl, then pile the mango slices on top. Using a teaspoon, dot little lumps of the "cheesecake" mixture all over the *bingsu* and serve with a generous scoop of vanilla ice cream in the middle.

TIP: Nowadays in Korea, *bingsu* often comes with a side of condensed milk, which you pour all over the top to make things really creamy and to add a little more sweetness. If you've got a sweet tooth, give it a try.

Soborro Cake

In Korea, *soborro* is actually a non-sweet bread, and one that I only really enjoy for its peanut-buttery crisp topping—I love to peel off all the crisp and eat it like tiny cookies. Here we've sweetened things up a little, giving it a peanut butter spongecake base and a buttercream filling to go with all that delicious peanut-buttery crisp. It's sweet with a slightly salty edge, and goes perfectly with a coffee.

SERVES **8 to 10**

1¾ sticks softened unsalted butter, plus extra for greasing
1 cup superfine sugar
3 eggs
¼ cup crunchy peanut butter
3 tablespoons roasted, salted peanuts
1⅔ cups all-purpose flour
2½ teaspoons baking powder

CRISP TOPPING
½ cup all-purpose flour
3½ tablespoons superfine sugar
½ stick cold butter, cut into cubes
1½ tablespoons crunchy peanut butter
1 tablespoon roasted, salted peanuts

BUTTERCREAM FILLING
¾ stick unsalted butter, cut into cubes
1½ tablespoons crunchy peanut butter
2 tablespoons confectioner's sugar
pinch of salt
1 tablespoon milk

1_ Preheat the oven to 350°F. Grease an 8-inch springform cake pan using a little butter and line the bottom with nonstick parchment paper.

2_ For the topping, add all the ingredients to a large bowl and rub the mixture between your fingertips until it resembles coarse bread crumbs. Set aside.

3_ In a large bowl, cream together the butter and sugar until pale and fluffy. Stir in the eggs, peanut butter, and peanuts and beat together until the peanut butter

is no longer lumpy and everything is well combined. Sift the flour and baking powder into the bowl and stir everything together to form a smooth batter.

4_ Spoon the batter into the prepared cake pan, leveling off the top with the back of a spoon. Sprinkle evenly with the crisp topping and bake for 45 minutes, or until a metal skewer inserted into the middle of the cake comes out clean.

5_ Meanwhile, put all the buttercream filling ingredients in a large bowl. Stir to combine until smooth and creamy. Set aside.

6_ Once the cake has baked, remove from the pan and transfer to a wire rack to cool. When it is completely cool, slice the cake in half horizontally. Carefully remove the top half and set it to one side. Spread the buttercream filling generously onto the bottom half of the cake. Carefully set the top half back on top of the bottom half and serve in slices.

Blueberry Mandu

A cross between Korean *mandu* and Polish *pierogi*, these crispy dumplings are filled with sweet blueberries. They smell just like pancakes as they crisp up in the skillet. I'd never considered eating *mandu* as a dessert before—I've definitely never seen them in Korea—but my friend Magda introduced me to Polish *pierogis* and put the idea in my head. With traditional *mandu* dumplings, we would usually fold the tops to make pretty parcels, which half-fry and half-steam, but with these it's better to crimp the edges with a fork, so that the dumplings can lay flatter in the skillet and get really crisp on both sides.

SERVES
2

1 tablespoon all-purpose flour
2 tablespoons superfine sugar
pinch of salt
1 cup blueberries

8 large *mandu* skins, either ready-made or homemade
(see page 24)
2 tablespoons vegetable oil

TO SERVE
Yuja Curd (see page 222)
vanilla ice cream

1_ Combine the flour, sugar, and salt in a mixing bowl. Add the blueberries, gently crushing half of them with the back of a fork as you go. Mix everything together thoroughly to form a paste. Set aside.

2_ Fill a small bowl with a little cold water.

3_ Lay a *mandu* skin flat in the palm of your hand, and spoon 1 teaspoon of the blueberry mixture into the center. Dip the thumb and forefinger of your free hand into the water and use them to fold over one side of the skin to form a semicircular parcel. Seal the *mandu* together by lightly pressing the edges with the tines of a fork, ensuring there are no gaps. Repeat with the remaining *mandu* skins and filling.

4_ Heat the oil in a large skillet over medium-high heat. Add the *mandu* and fry for at least 30 seconds on each side, until lightly browned and crisp (homemade dumpling skins will take slightly longer). Drain the *mandu* on paper towels and serve with vanilla ice cream and a tablespoon of *yuja* curd.

Hotteok SALTED CARAMEL-FILLED PANCAKES

Hotteok are traditionally sold as street food and can be found all over Korea. They're a chewy cross between a doughnut and a pancake, filled with a cinnamon sugar that melts to become a caramel as they fry. In Busan (where you can find the best *hotteok*), they add nuts and seeds too, and that's my favorite way to eat them. For the sugar filling to be completely melted they have to be served hot, but be careful because the inside can become molten. It's said that *hotteok* get their name from the "ho" noise made from blowing on them to cool them down. Don't forget to do this before taking your first bite!

MAKES 8 PANCAKES

1 teaspoon dry active yeast
1½ tablespoons superfine sugar
⅓ cup warm water
⅓ cup warm milk, plus extra if needed
1⅔ cups all-purpose flour, plus extra for dusting

⅓ cup sweet rice flour
1 teaspoon vegetable oil, plus extra for frying
generous knob of butter

FILLING
2 tablespoons ground hazelnuts

2 tablespoons pine nuts
1 cup soft dark brown sugar
3 tablespoons roasted, salted peanuts, crushed
pinch of ground cinnamon
pinch of salt

1_ For the filling, mix together the ingredients in a small bowl. Set aside.

2_ In a separate small bowl, mix together the yeast, sugar, water, and milk. Set aside for 10 minutes to allow the yeast to activate.

3_ In a large bowl, sift together the flour and sweet rice flour. Slowly add the milk and yeast mixture to the bowl, stirring together with a wooden spoon to form a dough.

4_ Tip the dough out onto a lightly floured surface and knead for 10 minutes until smooth and elastic, adding a few extra drops of milk if the dough is still feeling a little dry. Put the dough in a mixing bowl and brush lightly with the vegetable oil. Cover loosely with plastic wrap and let stand in a warm place for 45 minutes, or until doubled in size.

5_ Gently transfer the risen dough out to a lightly floured surface and knead for another 2 to 3 minutes to loosen it up again. Divide the dough into eight equal-sized pieces and form into little balls. Flatten each ball out in your hand to form a round disk, approximately ½ inch in thickness.

6_ Using the heel of your hand, make a well in the center of each dough disk. Spoon 1 to 1½ tablespoons of the sugar filling evenly over the center of each disk, then fold the edges into the center to seal in the filling. Gently flatten the dough again to form a ½-inch thick pancake.

7_ Heat the butter and a splash of oil in a heavy skillet over medium heat. Fry the pancakes one at a time for 1 to 2 minutes on each side, until crispy and golden brown. Drain on paper towels and serve immediately.

TIP: Heat any leftover sugar mixture with a little water to create a caramel, which you can spoon on top of the *hotteok* and ice cream.

My Mom's Miracle Cure

For as long as I can remember, this has been my family's go-to recipe for whenever anyone comes down with a cold. Its fresh, citrussy taste is quite strong. I used to hate it as a kid, though I've grown to like it as I've gotten older. I swear it'll get rid of a cold within 24 hours.

MAKES **2** to **3** MUGS

2 pears, halved
2 large oranges, quartered
1 lemon, quartered
1 lime, halved

3½oz fresh ginger root, coarsely chopped
4 cups water
liquid honey, to serve

1_ Put all the ingredients in a large saucepan over high heat. Bring to a boil, reduce to a simmer, and let cook, uncovered, for 25 minutes until reduced by about half.

2_ Remove from the heat and let cool slightly, then ladle the liquid into mugs. Stir in a teaspoon or so of honey to sweeten. Drink up.

TIP: You can adapt this recipe to your own taste. My mom's recipe is an adaptation of my grandmother's, and mine is an adaptation of my mom's. The key ingredients are whole, large oranges for vitamin C and pears to soothe a sore throat. The rest is up to you.

Ba-na-na Oo-You BANANA MILK

Whenever we visited my grandparents in Busan we'd take them a bag of their favorite treats, which would almost always include little bottles of banana milk. Bananas used to be really expensive in Korea, so when banana milk was introduced into the country it quickly became a big hit with both young and old. While I never really drink it in England—I'm not a huge fan of its artificial sweetness—I still always pick up a bottle when I'm in Korea because it brings back childhood memories. This recipe is for the ultimate banana milk, being an American-style, thick, ice-cream shake with lots of banana flavor. Perfectly ice cold, sweet but not sickly, it's just really, really great.

MAKES
1
GLASS

1 ripe banana
5 ice cubes
1 tablespoon malted drink powder (such as Ovaltine)

½ tablespoon soft brown sugar
2 tablespoons vanilla ice cream
⅔ cup skim milk

1_ Peel and coarsely chop the banana. Wrap the banana pieces in plastic wrap and freeze for 1 to 2 hours, or until needed.

2_ Put the frozen banana pieces in a blender with all the other ingredients. Blend together until smooth, then pour into a tall glass. Serve with a large drinking straw.

Busan BBQ

Since starting Busan BBQ in August 2012, it's been a bit of an adventure. We probably would have planned things a little differently if we had had more time, but we really wanted to get up and running for that summer.

Though it all started with a *Bulgogi* Burger, we felt like we needed to add a few other items to our menu before we started trading. We originally spent quite a lot of time working on the *Bulgogi* Burger recipe, but the ideas for the Pork Belly Bun and Korean Fried Chicken came pretty easily. Gareth was insistent that we include Korean Fried Chicken on the menu as it's one of his favorite things to eat, and we decided that three options would be good to start with in order to offer variety without stretching ourselves too thinly. Though we've tweaked our recipes a little since we started, these three are still the regulars on our menu.

We traded at our first market in North Finchley at the (now closed) North London Artisan Market. We had to make an early start since our trailer was kept a two-hour drive from our house (which was also a three-hour drive to North Finchley) and we had to be at the market for 8:30 A.M. It was a gray, rainy day and we were both tired from the long drive and early start. We'd thought we would have enough time to get our act together when we arrived. However, on that first day we still had all our kitchen equipment in its original boxes so we didn't know where anything was. We also hadn't prepared any marinades, sauces, or burgers, having planned to do it all when we arrived. Looking back, I'm not quite sure why we thought that was even possible. Our power kept flickering on and off and we were so behind and running around like headless chickens. Fortunately, we were lucky enough to trade at that first market with Nisha and Nishma from Grill My Cheese and Emily from Rupert Street who gave us so much help and advice on the day and we've stayed good friends with them since. From that first experience, we certainly learned that being prepped for a market is really important.

We'd hoped to join the guys at Street Feast ever since we started trading. Street Feast are the biggest night markets in London (though they now include lunch), with a strong emphasis on the best traders, food, and vibes. We were lucky because Adam from Street Feast visited us one day and tried our *Bulgogi* Burger. We were so nervous but a couple of days later he invited us to trade at the opening weekend of Street Feast that summer. To this day, that first day at Street Feast was probably the biggest highlight of our time trading. It was busy on another level completely, despite the fact that the weather was awful. People still stood in line and were amazingly patient, all having a great time huddled under umbrellas.

We've traded at Street Feast ever since. Street Feast makes sure all their traders are always thinking about developing their food and making progress. They've definitely pushed us to be at our best and to challenge ourselves, and we're thankful for that.

Apart from markets, we've also held a number of popups in restaurants and bars, such as a month at Gordon Ramsay's Bread Street Kitchen, for a Korean-themed bar. Popups give us the opportunity to be more creative with our dishes and experiment, because we're usually in a full size kitchen.

There's nothing like working in street food though because you have the chance to really interact with the customer. You get to watch as they take away their burger or fried chicken and take that first bite; when they close their eyes and start nodding, you know you've done something right. And the best part is when we see people recommending us to their friends. It feels amazing when someone has enjoyed our food so much that they want their friends to love it as much as they do. Seeing someone point at our trailer and hear them saying, "You have to try the burger from those guys. It's so good!" makes the long hours and hard work definitely feel like it's completely worth it.

Supplier

USA NATIONWIDE

H Mart

An Asian grocery store chain of 47 stores across eleven states supplying fresh produce as well as imported packaged Korean foods and housewares plus ready-to-serve meals. H Mart also offers an online service and delivers nationwide, but check the store locator on the website's homepage to find an H Mart near you.
www.hmart.com
toll free 1 800 648 0980

KimchiUS

This online retailer sells appliances, such as kimchi refrigerators, designed to provide the correct environment for storing kimchi and also meet various fermentation requirements. KimchiUS also sell electric rice cookers for serving 6 people or more, as well as the Homping Smokeless Charcoal Grill, which is small, portable, and suitable for use in the kitchen because it produces no black smoke or harmful carcinogens. They also sell karaoke systems. Free shipping within the US.
www.kimchius.com
(201) 482 4941
sales@kimchius.com

Koamart

This online supplier offers hundreds of authentic ingredients and groceries used specifically in Korean cuisine, including spicy Korean pepper bean paste, kimchi, popular Korean snacks and desserts, a variety of Korean seaweed and laver, Korean ginseng, and many exotic condiments and canned goods used in making Korean dishes.
3692 Grayburn Road
Pasadena, CA 91107
www.koamart.com
info@koamart.com

LOCAL SUPERMARKETS

Here is a selection of Korean supermarkets, but check online for retailers near you.

Asian Food Market

22 Green Springs Highway
Holmwood, AL 35209
(205) 941 1009

Goowha Market

14206 41st Avenue
Flushing, NY 11355
(718) 961 0999

Han Ah Reum

59-18 Woodside Avenue
Woodside, NY 11377
(718) 446 0759

Hana Mart

744 Millersport Highway
Buffalo, NY 14226
(716) 834 1910

HanKook Supermarket

1092 E. El Camino Real,
Sunnyvale, CA 94087
www.hankooksupermarket.com
(408) 244 0871

Joong Boo Mart

3333 N. Kimball Avenue
Chicago, IL 60618
(773) 478 5566

Ko'mart Marketplace

306, 2240 Royal Lane # 204
Dallas, TX 75229
www.mykomart.com
(214) 256-9000

Seoul Market

Stratford Square
1841 Eastern Blvd
Montgomery, AL 36117
(773) 478 5566

CANADIAN SUPPLIERS

Galleria Supermarket

Thornhill Branch
7040 Yonge Street
Thornhill, ON L4J 1V7
(905) 882 0040

York Mills Branck
865 York Mills Rd
Toronto
M3B 1Y6
(647) 352 5004
www.galleriasm.com

Seoul Mart

2010 Broad Street
Regina, SK S4P 3Y0
(306) 353 1551

H Mart Canada

H Mart has stores around Canada too. Visit the Canadian website to find an H Mart near you.
www.hmart.ca

OTHER ONLINE RESOURCES

Amazon

The Grocery & Gourmet section of Amazon is an excellent resource for obtaining hard-to-find ingredients.

www.amazon.com

Maangchi

Visit this website for all things to do with Korean cooking and cuisine, including a forum for exchanging information and ideas.

www.maangchi.com

Zenkimchi

Korean food journal written in English by Korea-based blogger Joe McPherson.

www.zenkimchi.com

Index

Acknowledgments

We have a lot of people to thank for helping us with both Busan BBQ and for this book, so please forgive us if we've left any names out—and be prepared for a long list!

Firstly, thank you to Cindy for giving us a chance at our first trading opportunity at North London Artisan Market and really believing in our food! Similarly, thanks to The Cheesers—Nisha and Nishma from Grill My Cheese—you made our first day trading all the easier by filling it with lots of laughs among the chaos.

Richard, Riv, Dave, Cecile, Alex, Abbie, Moses, and Gareth (the other one), thank you for helping us out in those times that we've needed an extra pair of hands, and to Jack for being our most enthusiastic and dedicated customer.

Shaun Searley, Allan Pickett, Neil Rankin—your advice and expertise over the past couple of years has really helped improve and develop our recipes, as well as filling our heads with lots of ideas.

Adam, JD, and the team at Street Feast/London Union—being part of Street Feast has pushed us to be a better business and to constantly evolve in the competitive world of street food. We're so thankful for the opportunities you've given us and look forward to growing with you and London Union.

Andre from Bluebird, Damon, Dan at Korea Foods, and the boys from the Quality Chop—thanks for keeping us stocked with supplies. You're the best suppliers we could ask for.

Mrs. Kim at Korea Foods, thank you for taking me under your wing. I'm not sure you've ever realized how much wisdom and knowledge you imparted to me. Your enthusiasm for cooking delicious Korean meals is really inspiring.

The look for Busan BBQ would have been very different without the help from the creative geniuses at Colt, particularly Alex and John. Thank you for helping us shape our vague ideas into a strong brand identity.

To everyone who has ever eaten from us—your support means that we're able to work in a job we love.

Anna at Johnson & Alcock—thank you for getting in touch and encouraging us to write this book. I don't think we would have dreamed that it'd be possible, but you've been so supportive and helpful in making this into a reality.

Denise, Yasia, Pauline, and the team at Octopus—we're so proud that this book has turned out the way we'd hoped. Actually, even better than we could have hoped, so thank you for your never-ending patience and for really listening to us.

Thanks to David and Victoria for creating such beautiful pictures and for Annie and Lola for making our food look so delicious. We hope the kimchi fried rice has become a favorite weekday dinner!

And to the final thank you to Umma and Dad—for your never-ending support, advice, love, wisdom, and everything else. None of this would have been possible without you.

To Noah

An Hachette UK Company
www.hachette.co.uk

First published in Great Britain in 2016 by Mitchell Beazley,
a division of
Octopus Publishing Group Ltd
Carmelite House
50 Victoria Embankment
London EC4Y 0DZ
www.octopusbooks.co.uk

Distributed in the US by
Hachette Book Group
1290 Avenue of the Americas
4th and 5th Floors
New York, NY 10020

Distributed in Canada by
Canadian Manda Group
664 Annette St.
Toronto, Ontario, Canada M6S 2C8

ISBN 978-1-78472-159-6
Printed and bound in China
10 9 8 7 6 5 4 3 2 1

Group publishing director: Denise Bates
Editor: Pauline Bache
Art director: Yasia Williams
Food photograher: David Munns
Location photographer in Korea: Ben Weller
Home economist: Annie Rigg
Props stylist: Victoria Allen
Designed by Grade Design
Assistant production manager: Caroline Alberti

Standard level spoon and cup measurements are used
throughout all recipes.

Eggs should be Large unless otherwise stated. The U.S.
Department of Health and Human Services advises that
some people, such as children, pregnant women, older adults,
and people with weakened immune systems or debilitating
illnesses, are at higher risk for a Salmonella infection and
should not consume raw eggs. This book contains dishes
made with raw or lightly cooked eggs. It is prudent for more
vulnerable people, such as pregnant and nursing mothers,
invalids, the elderly, babies, and young children to avoid
uncooked or lightly cooked dishes made with eggs. Once
prepared these dishes should be kept refrigerated and
used promptly.

Use whole milk unless otherwise stated.

Fresh herbs should be used unless otherwise stated. If
unavailable use dried herbs as an alternative but halve
the quantities stated.

Ovens should be preheated to the specific temperature—if
using a convection oven, follow manufacturer's directions for
adjusting the time and the temperature.

Pepper should be freshly ground black pepper unless
otherwise stated.

This book includes dishes made with nuts and nut derivatives.
It is advisable for customers with known allergic reactions to
nuts and nut derivatives and those who may be potentially
vulnerable to these allergies, such as pregnant and nursing
mothers, invalids, the elderly, babies, and children, to avoid
dishes made with nuts and nut oils. It is also prudent to check
the labels of pre-prepared ingredients for the possible inclusion
of nut derivatives.

Vegetarians should read the label when buying cheese to
ensure it is made with vegetarian rennet. There are vegetarian
forms of Parmesan, feta, Cheddar, Cheshire, Red Leicester,
dolcelatte, and many goat cheeses, among others.

JUNE 2017